Danah Zohar was born in the United States. She received her BSc in Physics and Philosophy from the Massachusetts Institute of Technology in 1966, and subsequently undertook three years of postgraduate work in Philosophy and Religion at Harvard University. She is married to a Jungian-oriented psychiatrist and is now settled in London, where she is a frequent contributor to the *Sunday Times*. Her previous books include *Up My Mother's Flagpole* (a humorous autobiography) and *Israel: The Land and Its People*.

DANAH ZOHAR

Through the Time Barrier

A Study of Precognition and Modern Physics

Series Editor: Brian Inglis

Published on behalf of the Society for Psychical Research

Granada Publishing

Paladin Books
Granada Publishing Ltd
8 Grafton Street, London W1X 3LA

Published by Paladin Books 1983

First published in Great Britain by
William Heinemann Ltd 1982

Copyright © Danah Zohar 1982

ISBN 0-586-08431-2

Reproduced, printed and bound in Great Britain by
Hazell Watson & Viney Limited,
Member of the BPCC Group,
Aylesbury, Bucks

For Ian

'If prevision be a fact, it is a fact which destroys absolutely the entire basis of all our past assumptions of the universe.'

J. W. DUNNE

'For us believing physicists, this separation between past, present and future has the value of mere illusion, however tenacious.'

ALBERT EINSTEIN

THE SOCIETY FOR PSYCHICAL RESEARCH

The Society for Psychical Research is the oldest learned society in this field. Its aim is to investigate apparently inexplicable phenomena scientifically. It organizes monthly lectures in London and other activities; it publishes a *Journal*, *Proceedings*, and *Newsletter*. An extensive library and archives are held at the Society's London headquarters where all enquiries, including membership, should be directed to:

The Society for Psychical Research
1 Adam & Eve Mews
Kensington
LONDON W8 6UG

Contents

List of Plates

Foreword

Around the year 1873, Frederic Myers was to recall in his *Human Personality*, a small group of Cambridge friends came to the conclusion that neither religion nor materialism has provided satisfactory answers to questions that were puzzling them:

> Our attitudes of mind were in some ways different; but to myself, at least, it seemed that no adequate attempt had yet been made even to determine whether anything could be learnt as to the unseen world or no; for that if anything were knowable about such a world in such fashion that Science could adopt and maintain that knowledge, it must be discovered by no analysis of tradition, and by no manipulation of metaphysics, but simply by experiment and observation – simply by the application to phenomena within us and around us of precisely the same methods of deliberate, dispassionate exact inquiry which have built up our actual knowledge of the world which we can touch and see.

Along with his friends – chief among them Henry Sidgwick and Edmund Gurney – Myers became one of the founder members of the Society for Psychical Research, when it was formed in 1882 to put these ideas into practice, and this series is being published to mark the Society's centenary.

The phenomena of the 'unseen world' to which Myers referred were originally for convenience put into five categories, each of which a committee was set up to investigate: telepathy, hypnotism, 'sensitives', apparitions and 'the various physical phenomena commonly called Spiritualistic'. Over the years the emphasis has to some extent shifted – in particular hypnotism, which at that time was dismissed as an occult delusion, was just about to be accepted as a reality, so it ceased to be on the psychic side of the fence. But broadly speaking, the phenomena under investigation are the same, and the ways in which they have been investigated have remained as Myers planned.

The terminology, however, has changed – and changed rather often, which made for some confusion. Myers himself introduced 'telepathy', as 'thought reading' was ambiguous; it could refer to the way in which Sherlock Holmes picked up what was in Watson's mind by watching his expression. 'Supernormal', however, which Myers thought preferable to supernatural to describe the class of phenomena with which the Society would be dealing, has since itself been replaced by 'paranormal'; and 'parapsychology' has been easing out 'psychical research' – though some researchers prefer to restrict its use to laboratory-type work, leaving 'psychical' for research into spontaneous phenomena. 'Psi' has also come in as an all-purpose term to describe the forces involved, or to identify them – for example, in distinguishing a normal from a paranormal event.

If evidence were lacking for 'parascience' – as it might now more embracingly be described, because the emphasis of research has been shifting recently away from psychology to physics – it could be found in the composition of the Society, from its earliest beginnings. There can be few organizations which have attracted so distinguished a membership. Among physicists have been Sir William Crookes, Sir John Joseph Thomson, Sir Oliver Lodge, Sir William Barrett and two Lord Rayleighs – the third and fourth barons. Among the philosophers: Sidgwick himself, Henri Bergson, Ferdinand Schiller, L. P. Jacks, Hans Driesch, and C. D. Broad; among the psychologists: William James, William McDougall, Sigmund Freud, Walter Franklin Prince, Carl Jung and Gardner Murphy. And along with these have been many eminent figures in various fields: Charles Richet, a Nobel prizewinner in physiology; the Earl of Balfour, Prime Minister from 1902–6, and his brother Gerald, Chief Secretary for Ireland in 1895–6; Andrew Lang, polymath; Gilbert Murray, Regius Professor of Greek at Oxford and drafter of the first Covenant of the League of Nations; his successor at Oxford, E. R. Dodds; Mrs Henry Sidgwick, Principal of Newnham College, Cambridge; Marie Curie; the Hon Mrs Alfred Lyttleton, Delegate to the League of Nations Assembly; Camille Flammarion, the astronomer; F. J. M. Stratton, President of the Royal Astronomical Association; and Sir Alister Hardy, Professor of Zoology at Oxford.

Such a list, as Arthur Koestler pointed out in *The Roots of Coincidence*, ought to be sufficient to demonstrate that ESP research 'is not a playground for superstitious cranks'. On the contrary, the standards of research have in general been rigorous – far more rigorous, as psychologists have on occasion had to admit, than those of psychology. The reason that the results have not been accepted is basically that they have not been acceptable: extra-sensory perception and psychokinesis have remained outside science's domain, in spite of the evidence. And although the prejudice against parapsychology has been breaking down, so that it is being admitted as an academic discipline in universities, it is still very far from securing a firm base in the academic world.

Sceptics have sedulously propagated the notion that psychical researchers believe in ESP, PK, apparitions, and so on because they long to believe, or need to believe. Anybody who has studied the Society's *Journals* and *Proceedings*, or attended its meetings, will testify that this is a ludicrous misconception. Many of the most assiduous and skilled researchers have originally been prompted by *dis*belief – by a desire, say, to expose a medium as a fraud. It has to be remembered. too, that many, probably the great majority, of the members have been and still are desirous of showing that paranormal manifestations are *natural*, and can be explained scientifically – though admittedly not in the narrow terms of materialist science, which in any case the nuclear physicists have shown to be fallacious.

No: insofar as a Society containing such a diverse collection of individuals can be said to have a corporate identity, it could almost be described as sceptical; certainly as rational, as this series will show. Not, though, rational*ist*. Unluckily rationalists, in their determination to purge society of its religious and occultist accretions, often failed to draw a distinction between superstitions and the observed phenomena which gave rise to them – which led them into such traps as refusing to accept the existence of meteorites, because of the association with Jove's thunderbolts; and to this day, they are prone to lapse into support for dogmas as rigid, and as ill-founded, as any of those of the Churches. If the series does nothing else, it will show how rationally – using that term in its proper sense – the writers have examined and presented the evidence.

Until comparatively recent times the existence of precognition, or prevision as it was more commonly described, was taken for granted. The Old Testament contains scores of prophecies, along with dreams (like Pharaoh's, which Joseph interpreted for him) which foretell the future. The Greeks in classical times had their oracles; the Romans, their soothsayers. Until the eighteenth century scepticism about the possibility of glimpses of the future was rare. But with the rise of scientific rationalism, prevision was left on the supernatural side of the fence, along with other manifestations of the miraculous. When cases were reported, they were put down to foreknowledge, coincidence, or invention.

Although in the first half century of the SPR's existence a great deal of evidence was collected pointing to the reality of precognition, it was not taken seriously until the publication in the late 1920s of J. W. Dunne's *An Experiment with Time*, Dunne's account of his precognitive dreams which, though they lacked the necessary independent attestation to impress the members of the Society, proved a hit with the public; and precognition has since enjoyed a measure of respect even from people who are generally sceptical about the reality of psychical phenomena.

Nevertheless objectors have continued to argue that extra-sensory perception of this or any other kind is contrary to what is known about the laws of nature. But physicists today are no longer dogmatic about these laws; in fact they prefer to use the less loaded terms 'models', the implication being that they are at best only an approximation to the reality.

Danah Zohar, who trained as a physicist, has surveyed the historical and contemporary evidence for precognition with a view to examining whether it can be reconciled with the current models of physics – much as Pauli and Jung explored the possibility of a similar reconciliation in connection with Jung's Theory of Synchronicity. As she emphasizes, the time has not yet come when there can be clear answers to the many remaining questions about ESP; but I feel sure that many a reader who shares my difficulty in understanding all but the most elementary physics will be grateful for the remarkable clarity of her exposition, which even contrives to make the technicalities readable.

Brian Inglis

Introduction

Each of us has an urge to cheat on Time. The same deep need which moved primitive man to consult witch doctors claiming to read the future in the patterns of blood flowing from the wound of a gored suckling pig, or which caused ancient Greeks to make the arduous journey to Parnassus to seek advice from the Oracle at Delphi, today moves people to read weather reports, tidal charts, or pre-election opinion polls.

With the wisdom of hindsight, we can see that ancient man may have been superstitious; but his arcane methods weren't always wholly wide of the mark. Much of the vision once attributed to the magical powers of 'prophets' and 'seers' was often due to primitive, but none the less skilful, capacities to analyse past events and project their patterns on to the future. Today we call our prophets and seers scientists or psychologists, and their methods of prediction are often very sophisticated, but they fulfil the same necessary function in our lives. In some sense, they all help us to look into the future.

Only the most dogged empiricist would deny the value and validity of predictions based on sound inference from past events or from carefully assembled data, but equally it would take a solid pragmatist not on occasion to want more. Most people at some point in their lives wish that they could simply crash through the time barrier and catch a wider glimpse of what the future holds in store. Throughout history, some people have been credited with doing so, and their reported experiences are the subject of this book.

Foreknowledge, prevision, or 'precognition', as the ability to see into the future is usually called today, is a difficult subject, no less so for the practised psychic researcher than for the layman. As Gardner Murphy wrote in *The Challenge of Psychical Research*, 'To make contact with that which does not yet exist is, for many, a contradiction in terms, a philosophical paradox, an outrage; or it even may be held to come under the category of "impossibility".' So that same mysterious ability which tantalizes us with its promise of granting a head start on destiny at the same time offends us with its outrageous and 'impossible' claims – far more so than any other psychic ability.

While telepathy and psychokinesis remain problematic in the absence of any hard and fast scientific proof that they exist, were such proof forthcoming it would issue no devastating challenge to our accepted way of looking at the world. The transfer of thought from one mind to another or the physical influence of mind upon matter require at most the discovery of some new physical force or some previously undetected capacity of the human brain. Either might peacefully coexist alongside the forces and capacities that we already know. But this is not true of precognition. Solid proof that some people do indeed have foreknowledge of events in the future would challenge the most fundamental tenets of both common sense and classical physics.

The whole rhythm of our conscious daily lives is lived out against the background of 'passing time', a succession of moments subdivided into past, present and future, and in this familiar structure 'now' must always precede 'then'. Allied to this is the law of causality, one of the most fundamental laws of nature, which states that a cause must always precede its effect. An effect 'now' could not possibly be the result of a cause 'then', and yet this is precisely what we are required to believe if we accept that some people can see events now although the causes which brought them about have yet to happen – a corpse before the person whom it was has been murdered, a newspaper headline before the paper in which it appears has gone to press, a devastated village before the earthquake which destroyed it has yet begun to send out its warning tremors. None of these things is possible according to science as we have known it.

'Foreknowledge of the future, of the detailed kind indicated in some of the narratives forwarded to us,' wrote one of the founders of the Society for Psychical Research, Frank Podmore, in 1908, 'would involve the shattering of the whole scientific fabric. If the things reported in some of these narratives really happened, we must set to work to construct a new heaven and a new earth.' Yet, while such universal reconstruction was perhaps too ambitious a task for a Victorian psychical researcher, it was soon undertaken by the new breed of twentieth-century physicists whose work has altered dramatically the whole conceptual framework in terms of which precognition can be viewed today. Einstein's Relativity Theory and the new quantum physics have wrought sweeping changes in both our scientific and our common sense notions of reality and each, in its own way, has stood our conventional notion of Time on its head.

In the world of relativity, there is no absolute sequence of moments, and thus no objective way of ordering events in time. Indeed, if some interpretations of General Relativity are correct, time may even be circular and journeys into both the past and the future at least theoretically possible. With developments in quantum physics, which take us into the shadowy microworld of elementary particles which make up the atom, the notion of any temporal ordering of events becomes even less tenable. Time itself becomes an elusive concept with no precise meaning, as does causality.

Curiously enough, while those who think about precognition are still embarrassed by its apparent challenge to the laws of causality, quantum physicists have learned to live with acausality as a natural outcome of their physical theories. The old categories of cause and effect have largely given way at the quantum level to discussions of acausal relationships which can transcend both distance and time. Even the once ghostly notion of 'action-at-a-distance', whereby physical bodies can influence each other despite there being no apparent exchange of force or energy between them, has recently been demonstrated in the laboratory. The widespread implications of such a breakthrough for understanding problems like telepathy, psycho-kinesis and precognition have yet to be worked out.

In fact, the tumultuous developments in the physics of this century have more than caught up with the 'outrageous' conceptual challenges once advanced by the shock troops of psychical research; and today much of the creative thrust within psychic research itself arises from efforts to digest and apply the new physics. Much of this book is devoted to discussing some of the more relevant ideas from Relativity Theory and quantum physics, and the whole of Chapter Eleven is given over to describing the new physical theories which attempt to apply these ideas to the problem of precognition.

The last century has seen a consistent effort to bring the benefits of science to bear on the questions which concern psychic researchers. The Society for Psychical Research itself was founded in 1882 by a group of eminent scholars who saw scientific discipline as a tool with which they might once and for all subject the murky waters of the occult to rigorous, objective investigation. The new 'science' of parapsychology, which attempts to study psychic phenomena under laboratory conditions, is one result of their efforts; another is the many attempts to understand the physics of psychic phenomena. Whether in the long run these technical approaches will tell us more about psychic phenomena than the patient and methodical collection of evidence from spontaneous cases which the Society for Psychical Research also continues to amass remains to be seen. Examples of both are offered in the pages that follow, to help the reader judge for himself.

Those who feel particularly close to the issues raised in the ages-old debate surrounding the mind-body problem may feel disturbed by the great emphasis placed on the physics of precognition in this book. As J. B. Rhine often observed, the importance of believing that precognition or any other form of 'extra-sensory perception' is indeed extra-sensory (i.e., non-physical) has played a key role in the emotional background of much psychic research, seeming to promise some evidence for the survival after death of certain aspects of the personality. But while some ideas from modern physics may one day help us to understand the mechanism by which a human brain can perceive an event which has not yet happened, there seems insufficient evidence in such understanding alone to argue that therefore materialism must have the last word on dualism. We understand precisely how the eye can see an apple sitting on a table, but it doesn't follow from that that we must go sightless into the next world; it simply tells us how we operate with an organ of our living bodies while in this world. For all that we know, the physics of the afterlife may well operate on wholly different principles.

Another issue that concerns many professional parapsychologists and those who study carefully the questions raised in psychical research is the extent to which precognition can be distinguished as a separate faculty, if it can be distinguished at all, from faculties such as telepathy (direct communication between two minds), clairvoyance (direct knowledge of some external physical source), or even psychokinesis (mind affecting matter). There are many who argue that all are just different aspects of the same strange phenomenon. Yet, despite strong arguments from experimental researchers like Louisa E. Rhine for equating precognition and clairvoyance, it will be shown in later chapters that such an equation raises difficulties for explaining how precognition might actually work. Such difficulties, though, need pose no obstacle to those who might equate precognition with telepathy or psychokinesis.

It may well be that an apparently precognitive vision of some future event is in fact just a form of telepathic communication with someone who already has knowledge of that event. Or, alternatively, it is possible that what really happens in precognition is that the mind 'sees' something (dreams it, imagines it, wishes for it) and then subsequently acts upon events in the world through psychokinesis to bring about the fruits of its own expectations. Each of the two main physical theories of precognition discussed in Chapter Eleven interpret the faculty this way – the one in terms of telepathy, the other in terms of psychokinesis.

In fact, there is no certain answer to either of these alternative suggestions, and there is not likely to be until a great deal more evidence for precognition becomes available and the actual physics of the faculty is thoroughly understood. Throughout this book it has been assumed that telepathy at least (and psychokinesis perhaps) must be very closely related to precognition, and cases of telepathy are mentioned whenever material related to them might help to shed further light on the nature and functioning of precognition itself.

Thus, psychological studies conducted to determine whether children are more likely to be telepathic than adults are thought very likely to indicate whether the same might be true for precognition, and therefore the evidence from those studies has been included. Similarly, while there is still very little information available to indicate whether animals have precognitive ability, considerable evidence suggests that they may be telepathic, and that evidence has been included on the assumption that it is relevant to understanding precognition.

Finally, it is important to say a word about the quality of the evidence cited for cases of apparent or alleged precognition discussed in this book. This varies from the extremely tenuous in much of the first chapter, where any supporting facts that may once have existed were long since generously interpreted to highlight mythical or literary themes, to the boringly rigorous in the case of laboratory studies of precognition described in Chapter Four. The vast majority of the cases discussed depend for evidence upon the corroborating testimony of reliable witnesses whose reports have been diligently recorded by officers of the Society for Psychical Research or in some cases by psychiatrists. Since it is still true that despite lengthy research efforts of many different kinds there is no hard and fast evidence for precognition of the sort that would convince an independent panel of disinterested scientists, I thought it best to include a full range of the kinds of cases that have contributed to discussions of precognition over the years. With the exception of the myths and legends of the first chapter, each case cited throughout the book is accompanied by some discussion of the evidence on which it was based.

I would like to thank my husband for his patient and invaluable help throughout the writing of this book, and in particular for his many ideas on the possible physics of precognition. Many conversations with Professor David Bohm have greatly improved my grasp, such as it is, of the implications of quantum non-locality and Bell's Theorem; and he was kind enough to read through the manuscript for purposes of vetting those parts of it which are straight physics.

And finally, I am grateful to the Society for Psychical Research for the generous use of their library and for the access they granted me to their research files.

A number in parentheses in the text refers to the source listed opposite that number in the Bibliography (pp. 168–72).

PART ONE

Is There Precognition?

1 Precognition in Myth, Legend and Pre-Modern History

If you can look into the seeds of time
And say which will grow and which will not,
Speak then to me . . .

Banquo, Macbeth

Banquo's wish for some vision that would give him information about his uncertain future is at least as old as recorded history, and until very recent times it was widely believed that such wishes could be fulfilled. The myths and legends of all human cultures abound with tales of shamans, witch doctors, oracles, prophets and holy men assumed to have the gift of seeing into the future. These visionaries were usually an established part of the social order, their mystic or ecstatic experiences a key factor in developing and maintaining the world's mythological traditions, and their services relied on by society's leaders in much the same way that today's politicians might seek divine inspiration in prayer or consult their paid advisers. The witches to whom Banquo addressed his plea are an obvious case in point.

Although the 'weird sisters' of Shakespeare's play are to some extent coloured by his imagination, there were two famous eleventh century Scottish witches living on the edge of the Thane of Glamis at the border between the counties of Elgin and Forres, and the real Macbeth was said to consult them frequently about the many intrigues which distinguished his troubled reign. It was on their advice that he built Dunsinane Castle, inside which they foretold that he and his family would be safe until 'Birnham Forrest came to Dunsinane' – a prophecy which he fatally mistook to mean forever.

Because of their reputation for reliable foresight, the witches played an important role in the day-to-day running of Macbeth's kingdom, as did their peers in other times and other cultures. Two thousand years earlier Saul, the first King of Israel, had also had recourse to the previsions of a witch. Disguising himself as a shepherd, he travelled to a village in western Palestine to consult the Witch of Endor, a local woman noted for having the 'familiar spirit'.

At the time, Israel was being set upon by the Philistines, and Saul had been forsaken by God and the prophets because of his enmity towards the young warrior, David, and his failure to obey God's commands. Asked by Saul what would happen to him in this crisis, the Witch of Endor called up the spirit of the prophet Samuel and through it, foretold that on the next day Israel would fall to the Philistines, and that Saul would be killed and succeeded on the throne by David:

> . . . for the Lord has rent the kingdom out of thine hand, and given it to thy neighbour David . . . Moreover the Lord will also deliver Israel with thee into the hands of the Philistines: and tomorrow shalt thou and thy sons be with me; the Lord also shall deliver the host of Israel into the hand of the Philistines.
>
> (I SAMUEL 28:7)

In the ensuing battle, Saul's three sons were killed and 'the men of Israel slain'. Saul himself was wounded by an arrow while fighting on Mount Gilboa and then fell upon his own sword rather than be tortured by the triumphant Philistines. David was soon anointed King of Judah, and later of all Israel.

The whole history of Israel as told in the Old Testament is so bound up with the spirit of prophecy that the cases recounted are too numerous to mention. Eighteen of the thirty-nine books of the Old Testament are subtitled 'The Book of the Prophet', and there is scarcely an event of moment in Israel's history that isn't introduced with the words, 'And the Lord spake by his servants the prophets saying . . .' and then concluded with, '. . . and it came to pass.'

In I Kings we are told that Queen Jezebel maintained no less than 850 prophets at her table, while King David made do with two official court prophets, Gad and Nathan. In Exodus Moses is served by one prophet, his brother Aaron, through whom God warned Pharaoh of the seven plagues which He would visit upon Egypt until the children of Israel were set free from their bondage.

It is Genesis that provides perhaps the clearest, and certainly one of the most often quoted, instances from the Biblical era of the kind of foresight most commonly referred to when speaking of precognition today – that of Joseph and his dreams. Joseph, who like Israel's other prophets attributed his gift to divine inspiration, accurately interpreted the symbolism of Pharaoh's dreams (the seven fat-fleshed cows, devoured by seven lean cows; the seven full ears of corn devoured by seven thin ears of corn) foretelling that seven years of famine would follow after seven years of plenty.

Through his foresight, Joseph both saved Pharaoh's kingdom from ruin and raised himself to the position of great power and influence that had been foreshadowed in two earlier, boyhood dreams, in connection with his family.

> Hear, I pray you, this dream which I have dreamed: for, behold, we were binding sheaves in the field, and lo, my sheaf arose, and also stood upright; and lo, your sheaves stood round about, and made obeisance to my sheaf.
> (Genesis 37:6, 7)

It was to prevent this and a similar dream from coming true that Joseph's jealous brothers had sold him into Egyptian bondage, an act which later led to the fate they had hoped to avoid.

This theme of Fate brought to fruition through acts deliberately intended to thwart it recurs in legend and literature, and of course lies at the heart of discussions about precognition and free will as the Greek legend of King Oedipus illustrates even more powerfully.

Told by an oracle that he would die by the hand of his new born son, Laius, King of Thebes, has the infant Oedipus placed on a deserted mountainside to perish. The child, however, is rescued and taken away to Corinth to be raised in safety by his foster parents, whom he believes to be his real family. In young adulthood, Oedipus is troubled by rumours that his assumed parents are not his real parents, and he visits the Oracle at Delphi to gain further information. The Oracle appears uninterested in his question, but tells him that he will kill his father and marry his mother. Horrified at the prospect of this prophecy coming true, Oedipus flees Corinth for the distant city of Thebes. On the way he murders his real father, whom he mistakes for a surly stranger; and then upon arrival in Thebes he marries his mother, Jocasta. Thus the oracle's prophecies both to Laius and to Oedipus are brought to fruition; as is the grim prevision of the blind seer Tiresias, whom the still ignorant King Oedipus has summoned to Thebes in hope of lifting the city's curse by discovering the name of his father's true murderer.

> A deadly-footed, double-striking curse,
> From father and mother both, shall drive you forth
> Out of this land, with darkness on your eyes . . .
> This day will show your birth and will destroy you.
>
> Sophocles, *Oedipus Rex*

The Delphic Oracle is, of course, the most famous seat of prophecy in the Greek tradition. Situated at the base of Mount Parnassus, at the point Zeus declared to be the centre of the world, the Oracle dominated Greek religious and political life from Minoan times until the rise of Christianity.

Few ancient Greeks would take a decision of any consequence without first making a pilgrimage to Delphi to seek guidance from the Oracle. The oracles were given out by young priestesses (Pythia) in a state of trance, in which they were granted a vision of the seeker's future by Apollo, God of Truth. Some students of the Oracle maintain that the priestess entered her state of trance by inhaling vapours which rose up out of a cleft in the rock on which she sat, others that she worked herself into it by auto-suggestion. However she entered it, evidence that the Delphic visions were achieved through an altered state of consciousness accords with modern data about precognitive insights, most of which occur in dreams or semi-trances.

Controversy surrounds the validity of the prophecies delivered through the Delphic Oracle, partly because they were often spoken in such cryptic form as to be open to almost any interpretation, and partly because the Oracle had become the focal point of the established religion of the times. There is sound reason to believe that a good many of the 'prophecies' were in fact bits of advice offered up by clerics who frequently acted as go-between in transcribing the priestess's messages. Not all of the many Delphic oracles quoted in ancient history and literature could, however, be dismissed so easily; and one example, involving Croesus, King of Lydia, recorded by Herodatus, is often cited as a case in point.

Worried about increasing Persian militancy, Croesus planned to consult an oracle for advice. But being a little sceptical, Croesus decided to 'test' various oracles by conducting an experiment (perhaps, as Whately Carington remarked, the first instance on record of psychical research) by dispatching seven messengers to seven different oracles, instructing each that on the hundredth day after his departure he should ask his oracle: 'What is King Croesus the son of Alyattes now doing?' The messengers were to bring him the answers they received in writing.

The answer brought from Delphi, and the only correct one, said:

I can count the sands, and I can measure the ocean;
I have ears for the silent and know what the dumb man meaneth;
Lo! on my sense there striketh the smell of a shell-covered tortoise;
Boiling now on a fire, with the flesh of a lamb in a cauldron
Brass is the vessel below, and brass the cover above it.

In fact, as his 'test' Croesus had decided that on the appointed day he would do something so absurd that it would be impossible for anyone to conceive of it through clever imagination or the normal powers of reasoning. He had taken a tortoise and a lamb, cut them up and then boiled them together in a hot brass cauldron which was covered with a lid of brass – an act which so precisely duplicated the words of the oracle that for once it needed no interpretation.

Although the oracle at Delphi was by far the most famous and institutionalized outlet through which Apollo expressed his spirit of prophecy, instances of individual seers being blessed (or cursed) with the gift of foresight are as numerous in the mythology of ancient Greece as they are in the Hebrew Old Testament. Two of them have continued to hold such sway over the imaginations of writers and poets throughout the centuries that they bear mentioning here: Cassandra, the ill-fated daughter of Priam, King of Troy; and the dreadful Sibyl of Euboean Cumae who features so prominently in Book VI of Virgil's *Aeneid*.

Cassandra makes her first appearance in the *Iliad*, but Homer has nothing to say of her prophetic powers, leaving this theme to be developed a few centuries later by Pindar and Aeschylus. It is in the *Oresteia* that we see Cassandra blessed by Apollo with 'the pain of grim, true prophecy,' which is doomed never to be believed because she displeased the god by refusing to bear him children. Cassandra foresaw the fall of Troy (including a vision of Greek soldiers hidden within the wooden horse), and later foretold details of her own and Agamemnon's deaths at the hands of the treacherous Clytemnestra, who in turn would later fall to the avenging wrath of Orestes:

We two must die, yet die not vengeless by the gods. For there shall come one to avenge us, born to slay his mother, and to wreak death for his father's blood.

Aeschylus, *Agamemnon*

After the fall of his city, the Trojan hero Aeneas set sail with the remnants of an army for the shores of Italy, and having touched on the coast at Euboean Cumae (a Greek settlement not far from present day Naples) at once made his way up the mountain,

> To the height where great Apollo had his throne,
> And the deep hidden abode of the dread Sibyl,
> An enormous cave; for there the Delian prophet
> Inspired in her the spiritual power
> Of his own mighty hand, revealing things to be.

Aeneid VI

Aeneas hopes to learn through the Sibyl's crazed utterances whether Apollo would lift the spell of bad luck which had seen the destruction of Troy and lend his divine blessing to Aeneas's plans for conquering Italy. In Virgil's description of what follows, we have one of the most vivid portrayals on record of the demented state that was believed by the ancients frequently to accompany prophetic visions. As the Sibyl spoke, she frothed at the mouth,

> Her hair rose on her head, her colour changed
> Her breasts heaved, she fell into a trance
> She seemed to grow, she spoke in no mortal voice . . .
> Out of a cave a hundred voices
> Poured out the Sibyl's prophetic answers.

Among these, she foresaw Aeneas's conquest of Italy, his wars there, his temporary refuge on the Tiber (at the future site of Rome) with the exiled Arcadian, King Evander, and the new calamity to befall the Trojans because of 'another foreign bride' (Lavinia). In addition she told Aeneas how to penetrate the underworld using a sprig from the Golden Bough, and just before lapsing into silence she foretold the imminent death of his friend Misenus:

> Meanwhile, though (alas you do not know it) the lifeless
> Corpse of your friend lying unburied taints
> The whole of your fleet with the odour of death, while you
> Loiter here at my door in search of oracles.

Returning to the beach, Aeneas found that Misenus had been drowned and washed up on the sand.

Compared to the rich and subtle Greek culture, with its abundance of poets and playwrights, the Roman world is often portrayed as being more pragmatic, more rational. But the Romans, too, had their prophets and soothsayers and a high regard for any omen that seemed to foretell the future, as is clear from the many contemporary descriptions of the events surrounding the assassination of Julius Caesar.

According to Plutarch (*Lives*), 'Before this event they say that strange signs were shown and strange apparitions were seen.' Unfamiliar lights and sounds filled the air, a crowd of men 'all on fire' were seen charging through the market place, the hand of a soldier's slave was seen to throw up huge flames, but when these were extinguished the slave's hand was unburnt and when Caesar himself was about to make an animal sacrifice, the sacrificial animal was found to have no heart ('a very bad omen indeed,' Plutarch observed, 'since in the ordinary course of nature no animal can exist without a heart.')

Suetonus (*The Twelve Caesars*) adds that among the 'unmistakable signs (which) forewarned Caesar of his assassination,' a group of the Emperor's veterans who had been sent to colonize Capua broke open the ancient tomb of the city's founder, Capys, and there found a bronze tablet with the warning inscribed in Greek:

> Disturb the bones of Capys, and a man of
> Trojan stock will be murdered by his kindred,
> and later avenged at great cost to Italy.

And according to Ovid (*Metamorphoses*), just before the conspirators had their way, arms clashed and trumpets were heard in the sky, the face of the sun was gloomy and drops of blood fell with the rain while a thousand statues wept.

But the two most familiar prophecies which appeared to foretell Caesar's impending doom were those of the soothsayer Spurinna, who warned the Emperor to be on his guard against a danger that awaited him not later than the Ides of March, and the vision which appeared to Calpurnia in her dream the night before the assassination.

As Caesar and his wife slept, according to Plutarch, the doors and windows of their bedroom 'flew open at once'. Caesar was awakened by this din, but Calpurnia slept on, talking and groaning in some inarticulate way. 'In fact she was dreaming at that time that she was holding his murdered body in her arms and weeping over it.'

Suetonius's account differs slightly. According to him, the night before the assassination Caesar himself dreamed that he was soaring above the clouds and shaking hands with Jupiter, while Calpurnia dreamed that a gable ornament resembling that of a temple – one of the honours (according to Livy) voted Caesar by the Senate – collapsed and that then Caesar lay stabbed in her arms. His version concludes, 'She awoke suddenly, and the bedroom door burst open of its own accord.'

Whichever account then, if any, that we wish to accept of the many strange omens and visions said to have preceded Caesar's death, there is at least no doubt that in the Roman mind this was an event thoroughly bound up with the forces of omen and prophecy.

'Second sight' was also attributed to the ancient Celts. With them, prevision was often described as just another racial peculiarity, like their red hair and moon-shaped faces. Their Druid priests were said to find prophecy so easy and natural that they had no recourse to the drugs or ecstatic states which were commonly employed by other peoples to enhance this faculty. The Druids, who spent many years perfecting the art of divination through apprenticeship to masters, were said to read the future in the flights of birds, from the shapes of clouds or tree roots, with the aid of bone-divining (using the boiled-clean right shoulder blade of an animal) or from rowan sticks. The best-known Druid seer of them all, of course, was the mythical Welsh magician Merlin.

So much is written about Merlin because of the key role he plays in the legend of King Arthur, and his many alleged prophecies within that tale are colourfully recounted by Geoffrey of Monmouth, and Sir Thomas Malory (and, most humorously, in the schoolboy trilogy of T. H. White, *The Once and Future King*). While there is no historical evidence that Merlin ever existed, his legendary powers of foresight are an important contribution to the myths surrounding precognition.

According to Malory, Merlin was responsible in the first place for the conception of King Arthur. When King Uther Pendragon, Arthur's father, pined for the Lady Igrayne, wife of the Duke of Tintagel, Merlin made a pact with him. In exchange for Merlin's casting a spell that would allow Uther to pass for the Duke of Tintagel, and thus gain entry to his lady's bedchamber, the magician required in turn that the child they should conceive that night (Arthur) 'shall be delivered to me to nourish thereas I will have it . . .' (*King Arthur and His Knights*, I). From then on Merlin is ever at the future king's side, as educator, adviser and prophet.

Among his Arthurian prophecies, Merlin foresees that Mordred, son of Arthur's incestuous match with his half-sister Morgause, 'shall be the destruction of all this realm,' and he later warns Arthur that it is dangerous to wed Guinevere because one day Launcelot will love her and she him.

Even as a child, according to Geoffrey of Monmouth's *History*, Merlin was said to have foreseen, through an allegory of two battling dragons, the Saxons' conquest of England and their eventual defeat at the hand of King Arthur. Whether this prophecy did indeed issue from Merlin as Geoffrey asserts or should, more likely, be credited to the imagination of Geoffrey himself, the events it describes do in fact bear a ring of historical accuracy. In Geoffrey's account of the prophecy, Merlin went into a trance and then spoke as follows:

> Alas for the Red Dragon, for its end is near. Its cavernous dens shall be occupied by the White Dragon, which stands for the Saxons whom you have invited over. The Red Dragon represents the people of Britain, who will be overrun by the White One: for Britain's mountains and valleys shall be levelled, and the streams in its valleys shall run with blood.
> The cult of religion shall be destroyed completely and the ruin of the churches shall be clear for all to see.
> The race is oppressed shall prevail in the end, for it will resist the savagery of the invaders.
> The Boar of Cornwall shall bring relief from these invaders, for it shall trample their necks beneath its feet.
>
> *History of the Kings of Britain*

But Merlin's prophecies are not limited to the timespan of King Arthur's own life and reign. According to Malory, just before Merlin's final leave-taking of Arthur's court, with the damsel who was to prove his undoing, he '. . . told the King many things that would befall.' And many of these previsions are detailed by Geoffrey of Monmouth in a chapter from his *History* entitled 'The Prophecies of Merlin'. Modern interpreters of these prophecies (e.g. 26 pp. 45–8) have claimed that Merlin foresaw the first Danish invasion of Britain during the reign of King Cadwallo and the second during the reign of Ethelred – and foretold that Ethelred would pay the Danes 'gelt' because he would be too cowardly to fight. In fact, the Danes demanded, and got, £10,000 and later £40,000, from Ethelred.

Merlin is also credited with foretelling the enthronement of James I, the Crusades and Henry VIII's break with Rome, but perhaps the most eerily accurate prediction attributed to him relates to Richard I

(Richard the Lionheart). Made 700 years before Richard's reign, Merlin's prophecy said:

> The Lionheart will against the Saracen rise,
> And purchase from him many a glorious prize . . .
> But whilst abroad these great acts shall be done,
> All things at home shall to disorder run.
> Coop'ed up and cag'd the Lion then shall be,
> But after suffrance ransom'd and set free.
> . . . Last by a poisonous shaft, the Lion die.

Richard I did indeed fight the Saracens, and during one of his later campaigns was captured and then set free. He died three days after being wounded with a poisoned arrow while capturing the castle of Limoges.

Up to this point, the stories of prediction and premonition discussed have been wrapped thoroughly in the many insulating layers of time, myth and legend. No doubt each one of them is a valid expression of some strain in the culture from which it arose, but there is no way from today's perspective of assessing whether or not any of them has any foundation in fact. Neither the visionaries, soothsayers and witches credited with these ancient previsions nor, in many cases, the events which they foresaw, necessarily existed at all or, if they did, quite probably not amidst the colourful circumstances which enrich their legendary existence.

With the next two cases, however, there is slightly more evidence for evaluation. Both the French Saint, Joan of Arc, and the French doctor, Nostradamus, lived recently enough for some hard facts about them to have been recorded, and each of them made predictions about events that history confirms really did happen.

Joan of Arc

Before her birth in 1412, there were said to be many prophecies which anticipated the career of Joan of Arc, and one of these is attributed to Merlin. Among his forecasts of 'things that would befall,' Merlin included, 'a marvellous Maid who will come from the *Nemus Canutum* for the healing of nations.' *Nemus* is the Latin word for 'grove', and *Canutum* is a medieval Latin usage meaning 'white' or 'hoary'. In fact, St Joan was born in a house at the edge of the Bois Chesnu in Domrémy. Bois, of course, means 'wood', and Chesnu is an archaic

French word meaning 'white' or 'hoary'.

Although Joan of Arc is remembered in history as one of the great liberators of France, her capacity as a prophet and visionary is a large part of the legend surrounding her name. Throughout her brief but brilliant military career she heard voices and had visions from which she felt that she knew what she should do and what the future held in store both for her and for her country. The voices and visions began when she was thirteen.

One afternoon while she was running through a field to join some other children at play, Joan heard a voice speaking to her from a cloud. According to a letter written by Perceval de Boulan-Villiers to the Duke of Milan, the voice told Joan that '. . . she was to do marvellous deeds. She had been chosen to aid the King of France, she must wear man's dress, take up arms . . . She was to be a captain in war.' Joan's military career actually began when she was seventeen, and that too was accompanied by a vision. At the time, she insisted she must carry out her mission quickly because, 'I have so little time. One year and a little more,' she said. It was just thirteen months from that time until her capture.

One of Joan's first recorded prophecies concerned a stranger she met soon after her enlistment, and she recounted the incident to her confessor, Pasquerel. Near the castle of Chinon she met a man on horseback who insulted her and swore at her. She answered him back by saying, 'In God's name, do you swear, and you so near your death?' An hour after this exchange, the man fell into the castle's moat and was drowned.

During the seige of Tourelles, Joan predicted her own wounding by an arrow. 'Keep close by me,' she told her comrades, 'because tomorrow I will have much to do, more than I ever had, and blood will flow from my body above my heart.' Again, Pasquerel confirms that she made the prediction the day before her wounding.

At the height of her military triumph in 1430, just after she had freed the passage of the Seine and opened the campaign of the Oise, Joan's voices warned her that her time was up. Soon after, she was captured, and during her trial several months later she made several additional prophecies; among them, a prediction that the English would soon lose their most crucial battle ever against France:

I know that before seven years are passed the English will lose a greater stake than they did at Orleans (in 1429, when troops led by Joan defeated them) and that they will lose all they hold in France. They will have a sorer loss than ever before through a great victory given by God to the French.

In 1436, the English lost Paris, and in 1439 they lost Normandy at the battle of Formigny.

Nostradamus

Three-quarters of a century after Joan of Arc was executed, another Frenchman whose name is probably more closely associated than any other in the popular mind with prophecy and prevision – Michael de Nostredame, or 'Nostradamus', was born at St Rémy in Provence. His allegedly extraordinary gift for predicting things to come remains a living (and somewhat haunting) legend in our own century, and among his disturbing prophecies are some which seem to have foretold the French Revolution, the rise of Napoleon and even, perhaps, the reign of Hitler.

Trained as both an astrologer and a physician, and deeply rooted in the Jewish mystical tradition (he was a converted Jew), the young Nostradamus first made his reputation as a doctor doing brilliant work during outbreaks of the plague in the south of France. His success in treating the plague was due largely to his insistence on the importance of fresh air and disinfectant when combating disease, though neither of these (nor even the existence of germs) was generally recognized until the nineteenth century.

While the more famous of Nostradamus's prophecies related to events that took place after his death, he achieved in his own lifetime a reputation for being gifted with the ability to foresee events: reigning monarchs and leading public figures arranged to have their own or their children's horoscopes cast by him. And while most of Nostradamus's predictions have come down to us through the publication of his *Centuries*, one early story relates to something which happened to him as a younger man. While travelling in Italy, he had occasion to meet a swineherd turned monk named Felix Peretti. Immediately, Nostradamus fell to his knees and addressed Peretti as 'Your Holiness'. Years after Nostradamus's own death, Peretti became Pope Sixtus V.

Centuries themselves, which were first published in 1555, are quatrains grouped in hundreds, and there are 966 of them altogether. Each quatrain is alleged to contain the vision of some future event. Their wording is strange, often riddled with obscure symbolism; and their vagueness leaves them open to wide interpretation – the main

charge laid against Nostradamus's predictions by people who feel that
a sufficiently deft interpreter could read almost anything into them.
Still, as Colin Wilson points out in *The Occult* (83), when the massive
body of the *Centuries* is taken as a whole, the large number of direct
'hits' scored by his predictions in the light of later historical events is
impressive.

As Nostradamus was a well-educated Frenchman, versed in the
political vagaries of his country and well placed in its society, it is not
surprising that among the more obviously meaningful and accurate of
his predictions, a large number forecast some later event in French
history. Many speak directly of the Revolution, though this was of
course not to happen until more than two centuries after
Nostradamus's death.

Two quatrains are commonly cited as presaging the Revolution.
The first reads,

> The city's leaders in revolt
> Will in the name of liberty
> Slaughter its inhabitants without concern for age or sex
> There will be screams and howls and piteous sights in Nantes.

Students of Nostradamus are almost unanimous in their opinion that
this quatrain seems to foretell the sadistic bloodshed and drownings
ordered by the madman Carrier at Nantes in 1793, under the auspices
of the Revolutionary Committee of Public Safety. Women and very
small children were numerous among Carrier's victims, and when the
children's necks proved too short to lay properly in the guillotine, and
that instrument itself proved too slow for purposes of massacring so
many, Carrier had the doomed unfortunates loaded by the hundreds
on to barges which then were deliberately sunk.

The second 'Revolution quatrain', generally accepted as foretelling
the deaths of Louis XVI and Marie Antoinette, is uncanny in its detail.

> By night will come through the forest of Reines
> Two married persons, by an indirect route; Herne the white stone,
> The black monk in grey entered into Varennes
> Elected capet, causes tempest, fire, blood and cutting.

In June 1791 Louis XVI and Marie Antoinette attempted to flee from
Paris by disguising themselves, he wearing a costume of grey, she of
white, and escaping through the Queen's apartments. They had got as

far as Chalons before being recognized by the town postmaster. They were arrested at Varennes, held for the night, and then returned to Paris to be beheaded. Louis XVI was always described as a man of 'monkish' appearance, and he was the first French king to be elected by the Constituent Assembly rather than to rule by Divine Right.

Nostradamus wrote three quatrains which have been taken for prophecies about the rise of Hitler and all the bloodshed his rule entailed. Perhaps the most often quoted is,

> Hunger-maddened beasts will make the streams tremble;
> Most of the land will be under Hister.
> In a cage of iron the great one will be dragged,
> When the child of Germany observes nothing.

Although subject to controversy, his 'Hister quatrains' ring true enough to anybody who accepts the validity of Nostradamus's prophetic powers.

Several of Nostradamus's prophecies seem to refer to events that might yet be expected to happen, and are of a generally disturbing tone. One, often taken to predict the end of the world, runs,

> Like the great king of the Angolmois
> The year 1999, seventh month,
> The Great King of terror will descend from the sky,
> At this time, Mars will reign for the good cause.

While most scholars believe the great king of Angolmois must refer to Genghis Khan, since Nostradamus frequently refers to Mongolians as the Angolmois, opinions differ as to whether the quatrain as a whole foretells a great war featuring hydrogen bombs, the overtaking of the world by orientals, or even an invasion from Mars. Perhaps we shall see.

Yet, compelling as most Nostradamus scholars find the evidence that his prophecies related to events in the French Revolution or World War II (or even the yet to be enacted future), one major new critical translation of the *Centuries* questions this whole approach to Nostradamus's work.

In his *The Prophecies and Enigmas of Nostradamus* (40), French historian Liberté LeVert suggests that in fact most of the events referred to in the quatrains of the *Centuries* are allusions to things that took place within Nostradamus's own lifetime – the retirement of the Emperor Charles V (instead of the exile of Napoleon to Elba), the political upheavals in sixteenth century Brittany (instead of the momentous events surrounding the later execution of Charles I in Britain), or events connected with the River Danube (the 'Hister' of the alleged 'Hitler quatrain'). Indeed, LeVert argues that when Nostradamus did try to prophesy more distant events, 'he was nearly always wrong.'

According to the noted scholar Dame Frances Yates (85), LeVert's new work has done both history and Nostradamus a great favour, 'providing for the first time a reliable text and translation of Nostradamus's poetry and sweeping away the trashy interpretations with which centuries of low-grade exploitation has covered it.' She feels that it is due only to LeVert that the real Nostradamus has at last been unveiled.

The I Ching

The last of the examples to be considered here as an instance of precognition as seen in myth and legend comes from the East, and really must be seen as a case apart. The *Chinese Book of Changes*, or *I Ching*, is one of the most remarkable creations (or discoveries?) of the human spirit. Though it is commonly referred to as an oracle, and certainly it does function as such, it would be a grotesque oversimplification of what the *I Ching* represents to see it simply as a crystal ball between hard covers. Yet it is for the book's uncanny access to the future that it must be included here.

The *I Ching* was compiled over 4000 years ago and has been used ever since by philosophers, politicians, businessmen and simple peasants who wish for insight and guidance about their future acts. The book contains all the combined wisdom of Taoism and Confucianism, as well as the sages who had gone before, and it is not content to present its seekers with simple, one-dimensional answers to their questions, whether about the present or the future. Rather, it places the questions put before it in a wider context than the questioner himself might have realized was relevant, brings out the nuances of a situation that were not present to his conscious mind, and offers advice on how best to confront the future experience which it foretells.

We owe it to Richard Wilhelm's sensitive translation and to Jung's keen interest that the book is now so generally known in the West. Like most westerners who first make acquaintance with the oracle, Jung's immediate reaction was simple amazement at the pertinence of the *I Ching*'s replies to his questions. Its insights were at times so startlingly accurate that he confessed himself almost ready to believe the Chinese myth that a living intelligence with whom one can converse actually inhabits its pages.

'According to the old tradition', he explains in his foreword to Wilhelm's translation, 'it is "spiritual agencies", acting in a mysterious way, that make [the *I Ching*] give a meaningful answer. These powers form, as it were, the living soul of the book. As the latter is thus a sort of animated being, the tradition assumes that one can put questions to the *I Ching* and receive intelligent answers.' Jung later tried to explain the mysterious workings of the *I Ching* in terms of his Theory of Synchronicity, as I shall be considering in Chapter Seven, but his sense of wonder never abated.

The *I Ching* itself consists of sixty-four numbered hexagrams which, taken together, are meant to embody the laws and nature of the universe and the rhythms of life within it. Each hexagram describes some almost archetypal element of life and is accompanied by commentaries which draw out the meaning of the individual lines. The lines which make up the hexagram are arrived at by tossing three coins (or allowing forty-nine yarrow sticks to fall) six times, and recording how they fall, concentrating all the while on the question for which an answer from the oracle is sought.

Most western people who consult the *I Ching* are unlikely ever quite to oversome their sense of incredulity (reaching at times almost the pitch of intellectual outrage) that it actually works. Jung was sensitive to this problem when asked to put his reputation at stake by writing a foreword to the book (34).

> I must confess I had not been feeling too happy in the course of writing this foreword, for, as a person with a sense of responsibilty towards science, I am not in the habit of asserting something I cannot prove or at least present as acceptable to reason. It is a dubious task indeed to try to introduce to a critical modern public a collection of archaic 'magic spells', with the idea of making it more or less acceptable.

It does sound impossible that by someone's tossing a few coins, his question can reach across the 4000 years of the *I Ching*'s past experience and receive some meaningful response about an event that is still to happen. And yet it continues to answer satisfactorily time and again for those who approach it with sincere questions.

Because the *I Ching* is meant to be studied and meditated over, and most of its responses involve the seeker in a complex and subtle dialogue with himself, to cite two rather simplistic examples of the book's 'precognitive' powers may seem to trivialize it; but they serve to illustrate briefly the point that it does seem to have some uncanny access to knowledge of future events, and thus is sufficient for my purpose.

In the autumn of 1978, a London couple were involved in the purchase of a new house. The whole process of agreeing the price, arranging a date for the previous owner's departure and getting their mortgage application approved was bogged down in complications and delays. At last they began to wonder if the purchase would ever proceed, and asked the *I Ching*: 'Q: Will our intention to buy the house at [address supplied] proceed with success?'

The book's answer was Hexagram 28, Preponderance of the Great. It read:

> PREPONDERANCE OF THE GREAT
> The ridgepole sags to the breaking point.
> Misfortune

The commentary added, 'The weight of the great is excessive. The load is too heavy for the strength of the supports. The ridgepole, on which the whole roof rests, sags to the breaking point because its supporting ends are too weak for the load they bear.'

A few days later the couple received a letter from their building society saying it couldn't approve their mortgage application on that specific property because it had suffered damage due to subsidence, and the society's surveyor had found major cracks in its support walls.

The second example concerns a feeling of great foreboding which overcame a member of the Society for Psychical Research the night before her brother- and sister-in-law were due to fly to Turkey. The woman became so worried about her relatives' safety on this plane journey that she got up in the middle of the night and asked the *I Ching* if it was safe for them to fly. It answered her in two stages because her first hexagram contained a number of 'changing lines' – lines which indicate the situation depicted in the first hexagram will give way to one portrayed in a second.

The first part of the book's answer was Hexagram 3: Difficulty at the Beginning. It read:

> DIFFICULTY AT THE BEGINNING works supreme success,
> Furthering through perseverance.

Nothing should be undertaken.
It furthers one to appoint helpers.

The second part of the answer given was in Hexagram 18:
Work on what has been spoiled. This read:

WORK ON WHAT HAS BEEN SPOILED
Has supreme success.
It furthers one to cross the great water.
Before the starting point, three days.
After the starting point, three days.

The commentary added, 'What has been spoiled through man's fault can be made good again through man's work. It is not immutable fate . . .'

A week later the woman received a letter from Istanbul in which her sister-in-law told her that their departure from Heathrow had been delayed several hours because, while their plane was taxi-ing for take-off, an indicator light on the pilot's intrument panel warned of a fault and the plane had thus returned to the terminal for repair.

2 Precognitive Dreams

> There seemed to be a death-like stillness about me . . . then I heard subdued sobs, as if a number of people were weeping. I thought I left my bed and wandered downstairs. There, the silence was broken by the same pitiful sobbing but the mourners were invisible. I went from room to room; no living person was inside, but the same mournful sound of distress met me as I passed along . . . I was puzzled and alarmed. What could be the meaning of all this . . .? I arrived at the East Room which I entered. There I met a sickening surprise. Before me was a catafalque on which rested a corpse wrapped in funeral vestments. Around it were stationed soldiers who were acting as guards; and there was a throng of people, some gazing mournfully upon the corpse whose face was covered, others weeping pitifully. 'Who is dead in the White House?' I asked. 'The President . . . He was killed by an assassin.'

These words were spoken by Abraham Lincoln to his biographer Ward Hill Laman in March 1865, to describe a dream which had left him so disturbed that, he said, 'I slept no more that night and was strangely annoyed by the dream ever since.' A few weeks later the President was assassinated by John Wilkes Booth.

Unlike much of the material from ancient legends, which was rather exotic by today's standards, involving as it did prophetesses, witches and the like, Lincoln's dream strikes a more familiar chord. Most people can recall having had vivid dreams and, judging by the testimony of some of this past century's great psychoanalysts and the bulging files of the Society for Psychical Research, some of these dreams seem to have foretold events which were yet to happen. Such dreams, diligently recorded and confirmed wherever possible by supporting testimony from a third party to whom they were related before the event foreseen actually occurred, make up the largest body of cases which might be considered evidence for the reality of precognition.

Thousands of apparently precognitive dreams have been reported to the SPR since its founding one hundred years ago, but most of these have had to be dismissed on grounds of being too vague or general, or for lack of adequate supporting testimony. Of the several hundred which remain, by far the largest proportion are dreams that seemed to foresee some traumatic episode – a death, an accident, or a general disaster, though some were simply dreams containing in vivid detail apparent foreknowledge of a trivial, everyday event. It would be impossible to relate every one of these dreams in detail here, but a selection should show what psychic researchers have judged worthy of consideration.

'Trivial' Incidents

According to his biographer (Forster, 1874), Charles Dickens once dreamt that he was receiving a visit from a woman wearing a red shawl who introduced herself to him as 'Miss Napier'.

'Why "Miss Napier"?' he asked himself on waking. 'I know no Miss Napier.' However, a few hours later two friends called on him, bringing with them a stranger whom they wished to introduce. Her name was Miss Napier, and she was wearing a red shawl (9, p. 179).

Summing up material collected by the SPR during the first fifty years of its activity, the writer H. F. Saltmarsh (64) cites several more instances of such 'trivial' precognitive dreams that appeared in early issues of the Society's *Proceedings*. In one, a Mrs Mackenzie dreamed that she was sitting in her drawing room with several guests, including a Mr J. She excused herself for a moment to check on their supper, and when she returned she noticed several black spots on her new carpet. Mr J. volunteered that the spots were probably inkstains, but Mrs Mackenzie replied, 'I know it has been burnt and I counted five patches.'

The following morning, a Sunday, Mrs Mackenzie told her dream to her family over breakfast, after which they all went off to church. Following church, the Mackenzies were joined by Mr J., who returned to their house with them for lunch, a thing he had never done before. While the family were chatting with Mr J. in the drawing room, Mrs Mackenzie went out to the kitchen to check on lunch, and on returning to the drawing room noticed a spot on the carpet. Mr J. assured her it was probably some ink and pointed to several similar spots. At that point Mrs Mackenzie burst out, 'Oh, my dream! My new carpet burnt!' The carpet had indeed been burnt, it turned out, in five places, by a housemaid who had carelessly dropped some live coals on it when lighting the drawing room fire (64, p. 55).

In another similar case Mrs Atlay, wife of the Bishop of Hereford, dreamed that while her husband was away on business, she had read morning prayers in the hall of the Bishop's palace. After them, she had gone into the dining room and come face to face with an enormous pig who was standing between the dining table and the sideboard. So amused was she by this dream that she told it to her children and their governess the next morning before reading prayers. After them she went into the dining room; there standing between the table and the sideboard, exactly as in her dream, was a large pig, which had escaped from its sty during prayers and made its way into the house (64, p. 56).

Although Saltmarsh himself took great care, as part of his examination of the evidence for precognition, to put forward all reasonable alternative explanations when looking at each dream studied, there is one possibility here that he seems to have overlooked. It is just possible that in Mrs Atlay's case, her prophetic dream might well have been brought to fruition through a practical joke on the part of her children. Letting loose the family pig in mother's kitchen, once inspired to do so by hearing such a funny dream, is the sort of temptation most children would find it hard to resist.

Premonitory Dreams of Death

When he was in his mid-twenties, Samuel Clemens ('Mark Twain') had a dream experience* that was to leave him scarred for the rest of his life. Thirty years later he wrote a long article on 'mental telegraphy' detailing the many such experiences he had had during his life, and from 1886 to 1903 his interest in psychic phenomena was such that he was a member of the SPR. He related the following dream to his official biographer, Albert Bigelow Paine.

Clemens and his younger brother Henry were both employed aboard the Mississippi steamer *Pennsylvania*. One night while the *Pennsylvania* was laid up in St Louis, Clemens slept at his sister's house and dreamt that Henry was dead. He saw Henry as a corpse, laid out in a metallic burial case supported on two chairs in the sitting room. On Henry's breast lay a bouquet of white flowers, with a single crimson

*If he is to be believed – Clemens was notorious for his wide-ranging imagination, in psychic as well as in other matters.

bloom in the centre. The dream was so vivid, that when he awoke in the morning Clemens assumed it to be true, and after dressing, went into the sitting room to visit his brother's casket. He was overcome with joy at seeing the sitting room empty and realizing that it was only a bad dream. He related the dream to his sister, and then did his best to put it out of his mind.

A few weeks later, due to staffing problems on the *Pennsylvania*, the two Clemens brothers were separated on their next voyage down the Mississippi. Henry sailed as usual on the *Pennsylvania*, but Samuel followed two days behind on the *Lacey*. When the *Lacey* touched in at Greenville, Mississippi, Clemens heard a voice on the shore shouting out the news, 'The *Pennsylvania* is blown up just below Memphis, at Ship Island. One hundred and fifty lives lost!'

At first it was believed that Henry Clemens had survived uninjured when four of the *Pennsylvania*'s eight boilers exploded, but then it was learned that he had been badly scalded and was expected to die. By the time his brother's ship reached Memphis, Henry was being carried into the dead room.

When Samuel Clemens went to visit his brother's coffin, he found it in a room filled with all the other victims' coffins. But whereas all these others were of simple, unpainted wood, Henry Clemens had been placed in a metallic burial case which the women of Memphis had purchased with a specially raised fund of $60. They had done so because the boy's striking face had raised special interest. As Clemens stood there looking at his brother's corpse, and thinking how like his dream except for the missing bouquet on Henry's chest, an elderly lady from Memphis walked up to the coffin and placed one there. It was a white bouquet, with a single red rose in the centre.

In 1812, a Cornishman named Williams dreamt that he was sitting in the lobby of the House of Commons when a man dressed in a dark brown coat decorated with 'peculiar buttons' shot the Chancellor of the Exchequer. Clement Carlyon vouches for Williams's dream in his own memoirs, saying that Williams woke, related the dream to his wife and then fell asleep again. While sleeping, he had the same dream a second time and woke so disturbed that he felt he ought to warn the Chancellor. However, friends talked him out of sending any warning and he let the matter rest until eight days later when he heard that Spencer Perceval, the Chancellor of the Exchequer, had been assassinated in the House of Commons lobby. Later, Williams saw an artist's impression of the killing, and the assassin was portrayed as being dressed exactly as in Williams' dream (32, p. 174).

On 16 December 1897, the British actor William Terriss was stabbed to death at the entrance to the Adelphi Theatre in London by a discharged member of the company who harboured a grievance against him. The night before, on 15 December, Terriss's understudy, Frederick Lane, had the following dream:

> I dreamt that I saw the late Mr Terriss lying in a state of delirium or unconsciousness on the stairs leading to the dressing-rooms in the Adelphi Theatre. He was surrounded by people engaged at the theatre, amongst whom were Miss Millward and one of the footmen who attend the curtain, both of whom I actually saw a few hours later at the death scene. His chest was bare and clothes torn aside. Everybody who was around him was trying to do something for his good . . . My dream was the most vivid I have ever experienced, in fact, life-like, and exactly represented the scene as I saw it at night.

Frederick Lane related his dream to Frank Podmore, principal investigator for the Society for Psychical Research and a noted sceptic about any matter relating to an alleged precognition. Podmore took the precaution of questioning two of Lane's theatrical colleagues, both of whom swore that Lane had told them about his dream over lunch on the day of the murder, several hours before it happened (57, pp. 353–6). 'It seems here,' Podmore commented in his report, 'that the dream-vision presented a fairly accurate and detailed picture of the event. The dream was not of the common type, and it is difficult to dismiss it as merely a chance-coincidence.' But while convinced that Lane's dream was genuine, Podmore was not equally certain that it was precognitive.

'It would seem possible,' he suggested, 'that the chief actor in the tragedy may have unawares communicated to some mind, which happened to be sensitive to its reception, the outline of the picture in which he embodied his desperate purpose,' – in short, Podmore felt that Lane's dream might be explained by telepathy between Lane and Terriss's murderer, rather than by any precognitive insight on Lane's part. Such telepathic communication is a common alternative hypothesis to cases of apparent precognition, though it is difficult to see what part it could have played in the following, much more recent case.

On 9 April 1975, a qualified social worker from Hull named Mrs
Lickness had the following dream about a man (Mr G.) whom she had
not seen for sixteen years. She reported it to Brian Nisbet, a researcher
for the Society for Psychical Research, as follows:

> There was very little in my dream, it was very clear. I was stood at one side
> of a not too wide room, a plain wall facing me. It was a light one, as light as a
> silver birch colour. The head of Mr G. was quite clear and appeared as if in
> sleep. I never noticed any detail of covering though. Someone was standing
> to the left of me, but in my dream I could not see who it was. I spoke and
> said, 'Oh! look, Dennis G. is where my Dad is now,' and that's all I
> remember.

The following morning, Mrs Lickness woke feeling perplexed by her
dream (she had never known Mr G. directly, only having seen him
from a distance sixteen years earlier when he called to collect his wife
who was one of Mrs Lickness's clients) and reported it to her husband.
Then she set out in her car to visit a friend, Mrs F. During the drive, she
stopped to allow an estate car access to the main road and was
surprised to see Mr G. behind the wheel. When she arrived at the home
of Mrs F., Mrs Lickness told her about the dream and about the
unexpected appearance of Mr G. on the road that morning – Mrs F.
herself was an acquaintance of Mr G. A friend of Mrs F., a
headmistress, was also present and heard Mrs Lickness's story. All
three felt that Mr G.'s appearance that morning, alive and well, meant
that the dream of his death was mistaken.

But unfortunately, as Mrs Lickness continued in her report to Brian
Nisbet, that was not the end of the matter (53, pp. 608–9).

> Bidding goodbye (to her friends), I continued on my calls for the day but
> when I reached home found a telephone message left urgently asking me to
> contact my friends. When I telephoned it was to learn that after I had
> pulled up, to let the man of the estate car out of the side road, he had
> continued to the town. At the traffic lights, in the centre of the town, while
> stopping at red, he suffered a heart attack and died there and then.

There were several witnesses to the various aspects of this case, all of
whom signed statements for the Society for Psychical Research.

Premonitory Dreams of Illness or Accident

The following dream would seem to be a candidate for supporting
Podmore's hypothesis that telepathic communication might serve to

explain certain apparently precognitive experiences. It belonged to a Russian doctor named Golinsky, and is reported in Medard Boss's influential *The Analysis of Dreams* (9, p. 182). Boss was a leading existentialist psychoanalyst and Professor of Psychotherapy at the University of Zurich, and noted for his careful investigations of dream phenomenology.

> I usually dine at three o'clock and sleep for one and a half hours afterwards. In July 1888 I was lying on my bed as I usually do, and I fell asleep at half past three. I dreamt that the bell was ringing and that I was being fetched to a patient. I then entered a small room with dark wallpaper. On the right side of the entrance there was a chest of drawers, and on it a peculiar sort of lamp or candlestick. I was extremely interested in this object. I had never seen anything like it before. On the left side of the door there was a bed in which a woman was bleeding severely. I did not know how I knew this was the case . . .
> Ten minutes after waking up (from my dream), my doorbell rang and I was called to see a patient. When I entered her room I was completely taken aback. It was remarkably similar to the room of my dream. An odd little petrol lamp stood on the chest of drawers on the right, and the bed was on the left. As if in a daze I approached the patient and asked her, 'Have you had a violent haemorrhage?'
> 'Yes,' she replied. 'How did you know?'

In this case Dr Golinsky himself wondered whether his dream had foreseen the future or whether the patient had by some telepathic means communicated her distress to him while he napped. He questioned her and discovered that her bleeding had begun at one o'clock, that she had become concerned about its severity by two o'clock, and that at four o'clock she had decided to send for her doctor. Thus the scene which the doctor had visualized in his dream was being enacted while he slept, and telepathy could therefore (though not necessarily) provide an alternative explanation to precognition in accounting for his dream.

Golinsky's dream is reminiscent of a much more recent one reported by British SPR writer Andrew MacKenzie (43, pp. 105–6), though in this later case the dreamer's attention focused on something of which the dream-subject was apparently unaware, and there is the interesting twist that the premonitory dream caused the dreamer to act in a way that bore on the future he had foreseen.

On a Saturday evening in 1964, a distinguished surgeon to whom MacKenzie refers as Mr Donald Wilson (a pseudonym), dreamt that he was seeing patients in his consulting room on the following Monday morning. The first patient to enter his room was a woman with a large discoloured patch on her right buttock. Mr Wilson could not see the patient's face, only her buttocks, but he was certain it was a woman he had never seen before. The dream impressed him strongly because he had no previous recollection of ever having dreamt of a patient.

Mr Wilson eagerly awaited his Monday surgery to see what would happen, but was disappointed when his first patient turned out to be a nurse from the hospital. 'So much for my dream,' he mused. It turned out, however, that the nurse had not been scheduled to see Mr Wilson that morning and had only been slotted in at the last moment. His first scheduled patient was indeed a woman he had never seen before, and while she was lying on his examination couch on her left side, he noticed a large, discoloured tumor on her right buttock.

'But it's two inches lower than I thought it was!' he exclaimed aloud, thinking of his dream, although this exclamation must have seemed odd to the patient, who had come to him about some other problem altogether. It was very rare for a tumor of that type to appear on the buttocks, and that rarity, together with his dream, drove Mr Wilson to conclude, 'This is too significant not to do anything about it.' Two days later he removed the tumor, which proved to be malignant.

'If I had not removed it,' he commented later, 'the woman would have died.'

Premonition and Prevention

There are many premonitory dreams on record which like that of Mr Wilson, appear to have prevented some dreadful thing happening by way of having acted as a warning signal. In the following three dreams, it was the dreamer himself who was saved through the agency of his own premonitory dream.

Towards the end of the last century, the noted American suffragette Susan B. Anthony was saved from a hotel fire by a dream. The incident is recorded in the diary of her friend and colleague Elizabeth Cady Stanton thus (59, p. 122):

> In a few days we are expecting Miss Anthony to make us a visit. She had had a very remarkable dream. The physician ordered her from Philadelphia to Atlantic City for her health. While in the latter place, she had a very vivid dream one night. She thought she was being burnt alive in one of the hotels, and when she arose in the morning, told her niece what she had dreamed. 'We must pack at once and go back to Philadelphia,' she

said. This was done, and the next day the hotel in which they had been, ten other hotels and miles of the boardwalk, were destroyed by fire.

Another such case was reported to the British SPR early in this century (60, p. 22):

> Mr Brighton, sleeping on board a yacht at anchor, dreamed of a voice warning him of being in danger of being run down by another vessel. He woke and went on deck, but finding everything quiet and in order, although fog had come on, turned in again and went to sleep. The dream was repeated and he again woke and went up on deck. He was rendered so anxious by the dream, and by the fog, that this time he went aloft, just in time to see, above the fog, another vessel bearing down on him. He shouted to the captain of this vessel who put his helm over and thus avoided a collision.

This dream is frequently cited in the literature on precognition. And while there is good evidence for its being a genuine case for consideration, at least one leading writer in the field, Saltmarsh (64, pp. 22-3), has felt it important to suggest an alternative hypothesis – that Mr Brighton, being an experienced seamen with the acute sense of hearing so often developed by men who sail, might well have noted subconsciously the almost imperceptible alteration of sound that comes with the lowering of thick fog and similarly the distant sound of an oncoming vessel, both of which could have been communicated to him in his sleep as a 'warning voice'.

Finally, there is the case of an English woman who was apparently saved from dying in an aircrash by a dream which caused her to stay off the plane concerned. This dream was reported in the London *Evening Standard* and double-checked by Andrew MacKenzie.

On 10 April 1973, a chartered Vanguard aeroplane crashed into a mountainside near Basel, Switzerland during a blinding snowstorm. The crash was regarded as particularly horrific in Britain because most of the 107 passengers who died in the crash were housewives from four Somerset villages on a day trip to Switzerland. Three weeks before the crash, one of the women who should have been on the trip, Mrs Marian Warren, a farmer's wife from the village of Churchill Green, had a dream which she later described as follows:

> It was all so clear in my dream. I saw the aeroplane come over some trees and crash into the snow. There were bodies of my friends being laid out. It was vivid and horrible. I felt cold all day despite sitting in front of a big fire. [43, p. 68]

Mrs Warren was so upset by her dream that she returned her ticket for the forthcoming trip to the tour's organizer, despite having to resell it at only half price. With the exception of one close friend, she told no one about her dream until after the crash, 'because I thought no one would believe me.'

It's largely because of a fear that no one would believe them, or often even a reluctance to believe themselves, that most people who have dreams which are possibly previsions of an imminent disaster seldom speak out, and if they act on their dream warnings at all, do so surreptitiously and usually with qualms. There is one case on record (43, p. 48) of a man booked to sail on the ill-fated *Titanic* who dreamt two nights in succession of her sinking, seeing himself as one of the victims, yet despite feeling 'most depressed and despondent,' couldn't bring himself to cancel his passage. It was only when his company cabled from New York asking him, for business reasons, to postpone his journey that he did so, and with a sigh of relief. But how many such silent survivors are there, whose lives were possibly saved through premonitory warnings?

In the early 1960s, an American parapsychologist named William Cox did an interesting survey which hints at some answer to this question. For several years, Cox collected statistics to discover whether people had a tendency to avoid travelling on trains that were about to be involved in an accident of some sort. Cox's statistics compared the total number of people travelling on a given train at the time of an accident with the total number travelling on the same train on each of the preceding seven days, and on the fourteenth, twenty-first and twenty-eighth day before the accident. His results showed that in every case there were fewer passengers in the damaged or derailed coaches of an accident-prone train than would have been expected for that train at that time. The difference between the actual number of passengers and the expected number in these cases was large enough that the odds against its occurring by chance were greater than 100 to 1 (80, p. 304).

Unfortunately, Cox's survey is the only one of its kind which has so far been published. The whole question of whether people do actually avoid death or injury through the agency of premonitory warnings is of crucial importance for its bearing on our later discussion of whether the possibility of precognition is incompatible with the existence of free will, and it is a discussion which would be greatly served by more hard statistics of the sort gathered by Cox.

Precognitive Dreams of Disasters

In the cases just discussed, the premonitory dream in each instance seemed to foresee some ill fate about to befall the dreamer himself, thus apparently affording him the opportunity to act on his dream if he wished. There is another large class of dreams on record in which some more general disaster is foreseen, a disaster not involving the dreamer and one which he has no means to evaluate or to act on until it is too late – usually after he has read about it in a newspaper or seen it on television.

Before the First World War, an eminent investigator for the American Society for Psychical Research, Dr Walter Prince, kept a written record of all his dreams. Among them was the following:

> Towards morning, I dreamed I was looking at a train, the rear end of which was protruding from a railway tunnel. Then suddenly, to my horror, another train dashed into it. I saw cars crumple and pile up, and out of the mass of wreckage arose the cries, sharp and agonised, of the wounded persons. And then what appeared to be clouds of steam or smoke burst forth, and still more agonizing cries followed. At this point I was awakened by my wife, since I was making noises indicative of distress . . .

Four hours after Dr Prince had told this dream to his wife and gone back to sleep, the 8.15 Danbury Express train to New York City was standing at the entrance of the Park Avenue tunnel, its front half in the tunnel and its rear end protruding. It was struck from behind by the locomotive of a local train with a crash of such force that it could be heard half a mile away. Many people were killed and trapped in the wreckage, and as one newspaper account reported, 'To add to the horror of it all, the steam hissed out from the shattered engine upon the pinned down unfortunates and rose up in clouds from the tunnel opening.' (50, p. 202).

A similar sort of dream was reported to British physicist Professor John Taylor (76, p. 79) in the mid-1970s, the morning after London's Moorgate tube disaster, one of the worst underground train crashes in the city's history. An underground train travelling at high speed ran past the platform and the front two carriages were crushed on impact with the dead end of the tunnel. Scores of people were killed or badly injured and hundreds trapped in the darkened tunnel for several hours. The professor's informant described a nightmare she had had the previous night in which she pictured herself in a tube filled with smoke. It was poorly lit, though she could make out jagged edges, and she could hear people screaming and sobbing. The woman told the nightmare to her husband immediately on waking, and Taylor said the words she later used in describing it to him were similar to those used by survivors of the crash itself – though in this case, as there was no written record of the dream before the actual disaster, such similarities could have arisen after the fact, the dreamer's dream-image recall being influenced by the very vivid descriptions of the actual crash that appeared in all the media the following day.

There is better documentation available to substantiate the disturbing dream of another Englishwoman, in which she apparently foresaw details of Britain's worst air disaster. It was on 18 June 1972 that a British European Airways Trident jet bound for Brussels crashed only minutes after take-off from London's Heathrow airport, killing all 118 people on board. The night before, Mrs Monica Clarke from Letchworth, Hertfordshire had the following dream, which she immediately related in detail to both her husband and her daughter. After the crash, the Clarke family reported Mrs Clarke's dream to Andrew MacKenzie.

> I dreamt I was with a friend – we were sitting on a seat in the country, although not far distant were tall buildings. The sky suddenly became darkened and oppressive. Without warning, there was a bright flash of lightning and an aircraft seemed to fall from nowhere out of the sky into a field very near where we were sitting. After a few seconds it seemed to burst into flames. Prior to this there had been no sound of an aircraft's engine. At this point I wakened. I was very troubled and shaken . . . [43, pp. 64–5]

While it may be mere coincidence, it seems significant that in Mrs Clarke's dream, 'there had been no sound of an aircraft's engine.' The Trident had in fact literally fallen out of the sky like a silent bird owing to engine failure – the engines had cut out and the plane stalled during ascent.

Finally, there is the Aberfan Disaster. At 9.15 AM on 21 October 1966, Wales suffered the worst mining disaster in its history. A coaltip located on the side of a mountain outside the village of Aberfan suddenly slipped, crashing down on to the Pantglas Junior School. 144 people were killed, 128 of them children from the school, which was partially destroyed in the avalanche.

The Aberfan disaster shocked Britain in a way that few other natural disasters ever have, perhaps because so many of its victims were young children. People from all over the country reported feeling horrified and sickened, many compared it to the Blitz and others said they felt a curious sense of personal loss even though none of the dead or injured were known to them. Having already noted that disasters often are associated with reported cases of apparent precognition, a consultant psychiatrist, Dr J. C. Barker of the Shelton Hospital in Shrewsbury, wondered if this one might be particularly so. He decided to find out, and in the process conducted one of the most thorough surveys ever undertaken of how precognition might relate to publicly known violent events (1).

The day following the tragedy at Aberfan, which had been the main item in all the British press and media, Dr Barker made an appeal through the science correspondent of the London *Evening Standard* for people who thought they had had any premonition of the disaster to write to him. Of the seventy-six letters he received, sixty seemed to him to merit further investigation (personal interviews, requests for corroborative evidence), and thirty-five of these were ultimately judged to satisfy his criteria for being cases of genuine precognition.

Dr Barker diligently recorded the thirty-five apparently precognitive experiences and classified them according to the amount of detail they had foreseen, the age and sex of the percipients, and whether the premonition had appeared in a dream, a trance, or as a waking vision. The vast majority were dreams, some of which were very detailed indeed.

One of the cases on which Barker reported involved the dream of a ten-year-old pupil at the Pantglas School, Eryl Mai Jones, who died in the disaster. Two weeks previously, this girl had spoken to her mother about dying, saying, 'Mummy, I'm not afraid to die.' The day before the disaster, the girl insisted that her mother listen to a dream she had had the previous night. When her mother protested she was too busy, the girl went on, 'No, Mummy you *must* listen. I dreamt I went to school and there was no school there. Something black had come down all over it!'

It should perhaps be said about this particular dream that, though no one in Aberfan expected the coal tip to collapse so suddenly or just when it did, the danger posed to the village by the coal tip was a matter of general local concern and had often been discussed. It is possible that this young victim was privy to such discussions, and they may have preyed on her imagination and affected her dream life. If so, her dream may have been a general anxiety dream linked only coincidentally with the actual disaster.

But no such alternative explanation is easily available in the other cases discovered by Barker. With the exception of that girl victim, none of the other instances cited in Barker's study involved people who had anything to do with the disaster or who lived anywhere near it. Most had never even heard of Aberfan. This was true of Mrs Grace Eagleton, from Kent, who none the less testified:

> I have never been to Wales nor do I possess a television set. On the night of Friday October 14 I had a vivid horrible dream of a terrible disaster in a coal mining village. It was in a valley with a big building filled with young children. Mountains of coal and water were rushing down upon the valley, burying the building. The screams of those children were so vivid that I screamed myself. It all happened so quickly. Then everything went black.

Neither Mrs Eagleton nor Mrs Mary Hennessy from Barnstaple in North Devon had ever had any connection with Aberfan or mining villages. Yet Mrs Hennessy's dream, which follows, contained even more vivid detail corresponding to the actual disaster:

> The night before the disaster I dreamt of a lot of children in two rooms. After a while some of the children joined some others in an oblong shaped room and were in different little groups. At the end of the room there were long pieces of wood or wooden bars. The children were trying somehow to get over the top or through the bars. I tried to warn someone by calling out, but before I could do so one little child just slipped out of sight. I myself was not in either of the rooms but was watching from the corridor. The next thing in my dream was hundreds of people all running to the same place. The look on people's faces was terrible. Some were crying and others holding handkerchiefs to their faces. It frightened me so much that it woke me up.

Mrs Hennessy was very upset by her dream, as she had two small granddaughters. None the less, when she called her son to tell him of the dream, she says, 'I told him it wasn't our two little girls in the dream as they looked more like schoolchildren.' She first learned of the Aberfan disaster later that afternoon, at 5.15 PM.

After analysing the results of his Aberfan premonition survey in detail, Dr Barker was sufficiently impressed by the number of cases it had revealed to wonder whether the apparent association between precognition and such general disasters couldn't be harnessed as a disaster 'early warning system'. He was instrumental in setting up a British Premonitions Bureau in 1967, and later a Central Premonitions Registry in New York City. The idea of such bureaux was to record all the cases phoned in to them of dreams, visions, etc. which seemed to be premonitory, and then carefully to compare these with any actual disasters which later occurred.

In the first six years of its operation, the British Premonitions Bureau received 1,206 reports of apparent precognition, some of which did seem to tally with later events (an injury to Prime Minister Harold Wilson; the deaths of fourteen children in a fire at a home for the mentally retarded; the death by suffocation of two young twins found trapped in a disused refrigerator), but no clear pattern emerged from these data. There was never any repeat among them of a flood of premonitions associated with any one single event, such as had distinguished the Aberfan study.

Dreaming of Winners

Scarcely a year goes by without some report in the popular press of a lucky punter who has won money on the Derby or the Grand National because he or his wife had dreamt the name of the winner the night before. Such stories are part of the mythology both of precognition and of these racing classics which so excite the public imagination, but on the whole they play little part in the considerations of serious researchers trying to weigh up the case for precognition. As Frank Podmore commented in the early days of the SPR, it is not difficult to imagine that the high hopes centred on such races would breed so many dreams that here and there one would be bound to coincide with the facts, while all the myriad of unsuccessful dreams would pass unnoticed. There is, however, one set of racing dreams on record which seem to merit more attention.

In 1946, Lord Kilbracken, then the Hon. John Godley, an undergraduate at Balliol College, Oxford had a succession of dreams in which he seemed to foresee the winners of various races. He shared his information at the time with a circle of fellow undergraduates, all of whom won money in consequence of his dreams and testified to that effect when questioned by researchers from the SPR. Thus the dreams, which are exceptional in their detail, are also well substantiated.

In his own report to the SPR (27), Godley wrote:

> On the Friday night, March 8th 1946, I dreamt what many would like to dream – that I was looking at the next day's racing results, with all the winners and prices written out in full. And in the dream I noticed that two horses had won which I had backed unsuccessfully on their last outing, and I remember being annoyed in the dream because I had missed them this

time. The names of the horses were Bindal and Juladin; and in my dream they both started at 7-1.

When I woke up, I remembered the dream, but of all the results I had dreamt I could only remember those two names: Bindal and Juladin. I thought no more about it till later in the day, when I happened to look at the morning paper and discovered to my surprise that both these horses were running that very afternoon. I told a number of my friends, who all advised me to back them; some of them backed them themselves . . .

Bindal was the first of the two to run. I bought my evening paper, and the first part of my dream had come true. So I promptly put all my winnings on to Juladin, which was running (as in my dream) in the last race; then I spent an uncomfortable hour or two waiting for a late paper. When at last it came, I somehow felt confident that I would win; and, sure enough, Juladin also had been successful. The two horses had started at 5-4 and 5-2, so that the odds for the double were $7\frac{7}{8}$-1, a figure very close to the 7-1 of my dream. My friends and I won over thirty pounds between us.

Godley reported feeling so excited by this outcome to his dream that for the next week he slept with a pencil and paper beside his bed, hoping it would happen again, but without result. 'After a while,' he said, 'I forgot the whole incident, and gave up hope that it would ever happen again.' A few weeks later, however, two nights before the Grand National (3 April 1946), he dreamt again:

Again I dreamt I was looking at the racing results. But this time, when I awoke, I could only remember one of the winners – Tubermore; and the next day there was no such horse running. But on the following day in the first race at Aintree, there was a horse called Tuberose; and the two names were so alike that I decided to take a chance. With my brother and sister I put on three pounds each way; and that afternoon Tuberose came in at 100-6. Between us we won just over sixty pounds . . . I had never heard of Tuberose before that day. It was an unconsidered outsider. I have watched its fortunes since, and it has never won another race.

The last of Godley's dreams in this succession (which included 10 dreams in all, in 8 of which he dreamt winners) happened on 28 July 1946. He reported:

This time it was different. I was in Oxford at the time, and in my dream I went into a certain hotel to ring up my bookmaker. It is my invariable habit to get the racing results from the evening paper, when I am interested in them, but on this occasion, in my dream, I decided to get them by contacting my bookie. I was smoking a cigarette, and the call-box seemed very stuffy. When I got through, I said to the man who answered me: 'This is Mr Godley. I wonder if you could tell me the result of the last race?' And his reply was, 'Certainly, sir: Monumentor at 5-4.' Then I woke up . . .

When I looked at the paper at breakfast time, I discovered that the favourite for the last race that day was called Mentores . . . The name, though substantially the same, was different from that in my dream. I decided that as, in the dream, I had rung up my bookie, I would have, in fact, to reproduce the conditions. So at five o'clock I went along to the hotel, and waited till the result of the race would be known.

At ten past five I lit a cigarette. Then I went into the call-box and put through a call to London. It was very stuffy in the call-box. At last I got through.

'This is Mr Godley,' I said. 'I wonder if you could tell me the result of the last race?'

'Certainly, sir,' he replied: 'Mentores at 6–4.'

Godley's case remains the best on record of anyone's seeming to dream winners, but whether his dreams were indeed genuinely precognitive is perhaps arguable. As a young man he was keenly interested in racing, and engaged in betting on his interest frequently enough to justify his retaining a telephone account with a bookmaker. Who can say what clues he might subconsciously have picked up while reading the form which then appeared as 'first impressions' in his dreams, or indeed how many dreams he might have had and then forgotten about non-winning horses? There was at least one other dream during that prolific period which he did remember, and which he sent to the Society for Psychical Research for possible later validation, but it was never fulfilled.

Godley and his friends certainly felt that he was on to a good thing with his dreams, but alas for them they didn't keep happening. He had one further experience in 1947, and then nothing at all for years. But in 1956, he received an unexpected letter from an astrologer, previously unknown to him, which set out in great detail why his precognitive dreams had stopped when they did and predicting that they would start up again in the following year. In fact there were no more dreams until the spring of 1958, but then they did begin to come again. Godley successfully dreamt the name of that year's Grand National winner, 'Mr What', and this was followed by other accurate racing dreams. But again, at least one dream filed in advance with the SPR (predicting that a horse named 'Neat Turn' would win the 1972 Grand National) did not prove to be accurate. Indeed, there was no such horse entered in the race.*

*Godley himself later said that he thought this dream had in fact referred to a horse named 'Gyleburn', pronounced 'Gill-burn'.

3 Waking Precognitive Experiences

In 1956, Dr John Peters (a pseudonym) was a young medical student sitting his second-year biochemistry examination at London's Charing Cross Medical School. One of the questions the examiners had set was to describe the synthesis of fatty acids, including experimental evidence for the different steps of the intermediate biochemical processes involved. Fatty acids are one of the end products of human digestion, and a basic building block of body fat.

In his answer, Dr Peters described several experiments, each of which illustrated some stage in the synthesis process. Among these was a crucial experiment showing that the first step in the synthesis was the binding together of separate units of the molecule acetyl-CoA (CH_3COO-CoA). This experiment, he added, had provided conclusive evidence that acetyl-CoA was indeed the starting material for the whole process (from a number of suitable candidates) through the employment of a double labelling technique: one of the carbon atoms (C) in the acetyl-CoA had been labelled with radioactive carbon–14, while one of the hydrogen atoms (H) had been labelled with deuterium (heavy hydrogen). Without the double-labelling, he summed up, it would have been impossible to determine which of the several possible 2–carbon molecules that appear as a first stage of digestion was the one which acted as the starting material for the synthesis of fatty acids.

Dr Peters was surprised when he got back his marked examination paper to see that, although he had received praise for his creative imagination, his professor had written in red ink beside his description of the double labelling experiment, 'This might well be a very good experiment, but it has never been done. There is as yet no proof that acetyl-CoA is the starting material.'

'But look here,' he said to the professor, pointing to his lecture notes. 'You described this experiment in your lecture during term – I've got it written here in my notes.' And there indeed was a detailed description of the double labelling experiment, and its conclusive proof of the role played by acetyl-CoA. But despite this, the professor assured Dr Peters again that he could not have said any such thing in his lecture because no such experiment had ever been done. There was, he said, an experiment in which a carbon atom had been labelled with a radioactive carbon–14, and there was another experiment in which a hydrogen atom had been labelled with deuterium, but neither of these experiments was conclusive, and biochemists were still in the dark as to which of the many possible 2–carbon molecules was in fact the starting material for fatty acid synthesis.

Dr Peters was left feeling very odd at the time. 'I wasn't accustomed to hallucinating,' he says, 'and in any case, there it was, written in my notes. But eventually I just forgot about it.' Eight years later, however, his memory was jogged and he was left feeling odder still.

'I was reading an article on fatty acid synthesis in a medical journal,' he says, and there was a report of the double labelling experiment I had described as a student, and the conclusion that it proved beyond doubt that acetyl-CoA was the starting material in the synthesis process. But this was a report of an experiment that had just been done for the first time, and it claimed to provide the first ever proof of the crucial role played by acetyl-CoA!'

Today Dr Peters is a member of the Society for Psychical Research, but he had never reported his student experience to the Society's research officers. 'I couldn't satisfy their criteria for proof,' he explains, 'because I didn't keep the lecture notes and it wouldn't have occurred to me at the time to have them witnessed by anyone else. But I am certain about the facts – it isn't the sort of experience I would forget.'

But was Dr Peters's experience a case of precognition? On the surface it would seem so. Its essential elements – a young student apparently 'day dreaming' during a medical school lecture puts into his lecture notes as recorded fact the details and results of an experiment that is only to be carried out eight years in the future – are reminiscent of many cases of automatic writing or trance-like prevision which have been witnessed and recorded over the years. Such cases make up only a small percentage of the whole compared to the large numbers of dreams usually cited as possible evidence for the reality of precognition, but the apparent glimpses into the future which they afford are often more precise or accurate, being unladen with the symbolism and displacement which so frequently distinguish dream life.

The Sinking of the 'Titanic'

On 15 April 1912, the *Titanic* sank on her maiden voyage to New York; some 1,500 of the 2,207 passengers and crew on board lost their lives. The disaster was a particular shock, not just because of the large loss of life which ensued but also because of the *Titanic*'s proclaimed invincibility. Because of the many new features in her design and construction, it had been assumed that she could not sink.

Not surprisingly in the light of research surrounding the Aberfan mining disaster, the *Titanic* incident too appears to have been foreseen in various precognitive insights. Many of these were dreams, but a few were trance-like visions or just plain 'hunches' that something sinister would happen to the ship. Certainly the most curious case concerned a novel written, apparently about the disaster, fourteen years before it happened.

In 1898, an American writer named Morgan Robertson wrote a novel call *Futility*, the story line of which centred around the sinking of a supposedly unsinkable giant of a steamship named the *Titan*. In Robertson's novel, the *Titan* meets her doom in the North Atlantic, during the month of April, through collision with a large iceberg. The *Titan* was carrying 3,000 passengers and crew, a large proportion of whom were lost because the ship had too few lifeboats on board: only 24 (the *Titanic* carried 20, also judged as grossly inadequate). There were other similarities. The *Titan* was travelling at 25 knots at the moment of collision; the *Titanic* at 23 knots; the displacement tonnage of the *Titan* was 75,000; that of the *Titanic*, 66,000; the *Titan* was 800 feet long; the *Titanic*, 882.5; and each of the ships was driven by three propellers.

A great deal has been made by writers on psychic subjects of the somewhat eerie correlation of details appearing in Robertson's novels and in the facts surrounding the actual sinking of the *Titanic*. One (23, p. 217) even goes so far as to claim that Morgan Robertson was a former sailor with no education, that *Futility* was 'dictated' to him while he was in a trance-like state seeking inspiration, and that an 'astral writing partner' helped him type out the novel. But other assessments are more cautious.

Dr Ian Stevenson, Carlson Professor of Psychiatry at the University of Virginia and a past President of the Parapsychological Association, did a thorough study of the seemingly paranormal experiences (nineteen in all) associated with the sinking of the *Titanic* (71, 72), among them the case of Robertson's novel. And while recognizing that, at first glance, the many points of correspondence between details in the novel and those of the actual event strongly suggest some precognitive awareness on Robertson's part, Stevenson argues that much of it might, alternatively, be put down to intelligent inference. After pointing out that there was much talk in the 1890s about the coming age of large passenger ships, he says:

> Granting, then, a penetrating awareness of man's growing and excessive confidence in marine engineering, a thoughtful person might make additional inferences about the details of the tragedy to come. A large ship would probably have great power and speed; the name *Titan* has connoted power and security for several thousand years; overconfidence would neglect the importance of lifeboats; recklessness would race the ship through the areas of the Atlantic icebergs; these drift south in the spring, making April a likely month for collision . . . Having reached the general conclusion of the probability of such a disaster, inferences, such as those I have suggested, might fill in details to provide correspondences which would have an appearance of precognition, but which we should, I believe, consider only successful inferences.

G. W. Lambert, a former President of the Society for Psychical Research, agrees with Stevenson's assessment (39), and offers the additional information that the author of *Futility* had studied form in the shipping world and was knowledgeable enough about ship design to speculate about future developments in the field.

Two other examples of what appear to be waking precognitive experiences associated with the *Titanic* disaster are not as readily dismissed. One is a 'vision', and the other a 'hunch'.

On 10 April 1912, the day the *Titanic* left Southampton Docks for her journey to America, Mrs Jack Marshall was watching the ship's progress from the roof of her house as it passed through the narrow body of water separating England from the Isle of Wight. Suddenly Mrs Marshall turned to her family, who were watching with her, and in a very agitated state said:

> That ship is going to sink before it reaches America . . . Don't stand there staring at me! Do something! You fools, I can see hundreds of people struggling in the icy water! Are you all so blind that you are going to let them drown?

Despite assurances from her family that the *Titanic* was unsinkable, Mrs Marshall would not be calmed, and she remained in an agitated state until five days later when her warning vision was fulfilled (43, p. 47).

A 'hunch' associated with the *Titanic*'s sinking was a life-saving sense of foreboding that was sufficiently strong to make a young man turn down a better career prospect rather than sail with the ship on her maiden voyage. Mr Colin Macdonald, a thirty-three-year-old ship's engineer was offered the post of second engineer on the new wonder ship, but despite the offer's representing a considerable promotion for him, Macdonald turned it down. The offer was repeated three times, but he consistently refused. The man who did eventually accept the position in his stead lost his life when the ship sank (72).

A Seance Prediction

Several of the paranormal experiences associated with the *Titanic* that were studied by Dr Stevenson in his survey had been had by 'sensitives' or clairvoyants, who had had visions of a sinking ship or of some disaster at sea just a few days before the tragedy. Such reputedly gifted people are often mentioned in connection with waking precognitive experiences, frequently delivering their forevisions at seances arranged for that purpose. Frank Podmore, while finding that the credibility of many seance predictions was inconclusive, reported on one case which he felt to be particularly well documented.

An English woman recently arrived in Boston, identified as Mrs P., was taken to visit a clairvoyant medium by William Lloyd Garrison, the famous Abolitionist. In Mrs P.'s account, the following happened:

> Though I had only arrived in Boston the day before, her guides instantly recognized that I came over the water, and opened up, not only my past life, but a great deal of the future. They said I had a picture of my family with me, and on my producing it, the medium told me (in trance) that two of my children were in the spirit world, and, pointing to one son in the group, she said: 'You will soon have this one there; he will die suddenly, – but you must not weep for him; he will be taken from the evil to come. It is not often permitted to tell these things, but we see it is best for you, that you may know it is no accident.'
>
> I had not been home many weeks, before my son, a brave boy of seventeen, was killed at a game of football. [58, p. 349]

More modern cases of seance room predictions appear from time to time in books and newspapers on psychic subjects, but as so many mediums have been caught out in rank fraud, and few have consented to a rigorous investigation of their practices, judgement must be reserved before accepting their prognostications as evidence for any genuine precognitive ability.

Trance-Like Previsions

When Goethe was twenty-two years old and had just taken leave of Fredericka Brion, with whom he was in love, he appears spontaneously to have fallen into the sort of trance usually associated with mediums, during which he had what might have been a precognitive vision. He recalled the experience in *Dichtung und Wahrheit*.

> I now rode on horseback over the footpath to Drusenheim, when one of the strangest experiences befell me. Not with the eyes of the body, but with those of the spirit, I saw myself on horseback coming towards me on the same path dressed in a suit such as I had never worn, pale-grey with some gold. As soon as I had shaken myself out of the reverie the form vanished. It is strange, however, that I found myself returning on the same path eight years afterward to visit Fredericka once more and that I then wore the suit I had dreamt of, and this not by design but by chance . . . Be this as it may, the strange phantasm had a calming influence on my feelings in those moments following the parting.

In Goethe's case, of course, there is only his word for it that he had the reported vision, and no way of establishing now what role any subconscious memory of the vision might later have played in his selection of a suit to wear for his reunion with Fredericka. But since the founding of the Society for Psychical Research, many similar visions have been reported, and a proportion of these has been supported by independent testimony and then fully researched.

Frank Podmore reported on the case of a Mrs McAlpine from Glasgow who had what might have been a precognitive vision while in a trance-like state. While waiting for a train at Castleblaney, Mrs McAlpine sat down on a rock by some water and gave herself up completely to appreciating the strong sunshine and the beauty of the landscape around her. But soon her idyllic state was disturbed:

> There was not a sound or movement, except the soft ripple of the water on the sand at my feet. Presently I felt a cold chill creep through me, and a curious stiffness of my limbs, as if I *could* not move, though wishing to do so. I felt frightened, yet chained to the spot, and as if impelled to stare at the water straight in front of me. Gradually a black cloud seemed to rise, and in the midst of it I saw a tall man in a suit of tweed, jump in the water and sink.
>
> In a moment the darkness was gone, and I again became sensible of the heat and sunshine, but I was awed and felt 'eerie'.

A few days after Mrs McAlpine's vision, a bank clerk did commit suicide by jumping into the water just where she had been sitting, though Podmore sounds a note of caution about what conclusions to draw from this chain of events. As in the seemingly precognitive dream of Frederick Lane the night before the actor William Terriss was murdered, which I have cited earlier, Podmore thinks Mrs McAlpine's apparently premonitory vision may possibly have been a case of telepathy rather than of precognition – assuming the strong possibility that the suicidal bank clerk had been dwelling on his own end for a few days in advance.

The possibility that telepathy might serve to explain many of the spontaneous occurrences which on first sight seem precognitive is raised frequently by serious writers in the field, and should always be borne in mind (along with subconscious inference) as an alternative hypothesis to proof for the existence of precognition.* But there keep being cases which, if as well founded as they seem, don't easily fit into any alternative model. Some of those associated with the Aberfan mining disaster illustrate this.

On 21 October 1966, the day before the Aberfan disaster, Mrs Constance Milder of Devon claimed to have seen the disaster in a waking vision.

> First I 'saw' an old school house nestling in a valley, then a Welsh miner, then an avalanche of coal hurtling down a mountainside. At the bottom of the mountain of hurtling coal was a little boy with a long fringe looking absolutely terrified to death. Then for quite a while I 'saw' rescue operations taking place. I had an impression that the little boy was left behind and saved. He looked so grief stricken. I could never forget him, and also with him was one of the rescuers wearing an unusual peaked cap.

Mrs Milder shared her vision with six witnesses at a Private Circle Meeting of her Spiritualist church, and also talked about it to her next door neighbour before either saw the television news broadcast which reported the disaster. In fact, details of that broadcast brought to light an interesting special twist in Mrs Milder's vision.

'Now this is probably stranger still,' she wrote to Dr Barker when she reported her vision to him. 'Whilst looking at "The Mountain That Moved" on television, on Sunday evening, I saw both the terrified

---

*There is also some vogue, particularly among recent writers, to include psychokinesis (PK) as an alternative hypothesis to precognition, suggesting that the mind of the percipient somehow brings about the fulfilment of its own previsions; but this may raise more problems than it hopes to solve.

little boy talking to a reporter and also the rescuer I had seen in my "visions".' (1, p. 173) Barker observed that many of the confirmed cases of apparent precognition reported to him involved the percipient, whether dreamer or visionary, being able to detect images from his precognitive experiences in the television pictures or newspaper photographs which later reported the disaster. Other researchers have also commented on the frequent correspondence between precognitive images and publicly broadcast or printed images which later appear, and this correspondence will be important in later attempts to understand how precognition might work.

Two weeks before the Aberfan disaster, another Spiritualist, a lady from Coventry, stood up at a 'Home Development Circle' Meeting, moaning, distressed, and wringing her hands, and said,

> . . . Something coming from the ground . . . earth . . . dear little bodies . . . I can hear water . . . very, very cold . . . never happened before . . . you will all be shocked . . . need never happen . . . those men dabbling with nature . . . they don't understand what harm they are doing . . . will shock the whole nation . . .

The woman herself was in a state of deep trance* when she uttered these words, but several others present reported them to Dr Barker and felt certain they must relate to Aberfan.

Premonitory Scripts

This last case from the Aberfan study was less articulate and contained fewer definite details of the sort which usually distinguish precognitive dreams or visions. It seems, after the fact, to have been a prevision of Aberfan, because of certain tantalizing phrases ('dear little bodies', 'dabbling with nature'), but in its vagueness and openness to interpretation, it is more reminiscent of some of the Delphic oracles or of Nostradamus's prophecies than of most modern cases of precognitive vision. The same is also true of certain 'automatic scripts' which have been handed over to the SPR from time to time in this century. Though vague, and sometimes ripe with symbolism, they often contain key images, words or phrases which make them worthy of serious consideration as possible instances of precognition.

The case of Mrs Verrall is often cited in the literature of psychic

---

*As a rule, seances involve the induction of trance states, the significance of which for precognition is discussed in Chapter Six.

research. Mrs Verrall, a classics don at Cambridge, was one of a group of eminent people at the turn of the century associated with a project which came to be known as the 'Cross Correspondences' and existed to study the possibility of communicating with the dead. (Dr Alan Gauld discusses their results in another book in this series, *Mediumship and Survival: A Century of Investigations*.) She was noted for her gift of automatic writing – taking down messages, while in trance, which were thought to be dictated by a purported communicator who was dead. On 11 December 1901, Mrs Verrall wrote:

> Nothing too mean the trivial helps, gives confidence. Hence this. Frost and a candle in the dim light. Marmontel. He was reading on a sofa or bed – there was only a candle's light. She will surely remember this. The book was lent, not his own – he talked about it.

On 17 December, she wrote:

> Marmontel is right. It was a French book, a memoir, I think. Passy may help, Souvenirs de Passy or Fleury. Marmontel was not on the cover – the book was bound and it was lent – two volumes in old-fashioned binding and print. It is not in any papers – it is an attempt to make someone remember – an incident.

Two and a half months later, Mrs Verrall's friend Mr Marsh came to dinner. He mentioned that he had recently (on 20 and 21 February) been reading *Marmontel's Memoirs* during a visit to Paris. He said that he had borrowed the book, one of three volumes, from the London Library and in Paris had read it lying down (on 20 February in bed; on 21 February lying between two chairs), by the light of a candle. There was no frost in Paris, but he said it had been very cold. Like most books from the London Library, the book was bound, not in modern binding, and the name Marmontel was on the back. When Mrs Verrall asked Mr Marsh if 'Passy' or 'Fleury' had anything to do with his reading of Marmontel, he was able to recall that in a passage he had read on 21 February, there was a description of a panel at Passy and that the panel was connected with a story in which Fleury plays a large part.

Although there are a few discrepancies between the details related in Mrs Verrall's script and those actually connected with Mr Marsh's Paris reading, her script does appear to contain an uncanny prevision of that reading. She had posted her script to an independent researcher, Mrs Sidgwick of the SPR, before meeting Mr Marsh for dinner in the spring and learning about his reading (57, pp. 358–9).

Playwright and writer Dame Edith Lyttelton was also a member of the SPR and, writing under the pseudonym 'Mrs King', she submitted many automatic scripts for assessment to a group of interpreters which included the second Earl Balfour, the physicist Sir Oliver Lodge, and J. G. Piddington, Joint Secretary of the SPR. Quoting her purported communicator, Dame Edith wrote down scripts which seemed to foretell such things as the sinking of the *Lusitania* (which was torpedoed by a German U-Boat in 1915, costing some 1,200 lives), the Treaty of Munich which left Czechoslovakia open to German invasion at the start of World War II, and the advent of that war itself – with an indirect reference to Hitler.

In February 1914, Dame Edith wrote, 'Lusitania foam and fire – mest [sic] the funnel – in broken arcs . . .', and in May that year she added, '. . . open your ear to the unknown – fear is the arch enemy. Lusitania.' The *Lusitania* was sunk in May 1915, by a single torpedo on the starboard side, just behind the bridge. On impact, the torpedo detonated the ship's cargo of 4,200 cases of rifle ammunition, setting the ship on fire and sending a huge cloud of smoke up over the funnel.

Andrew MacKenzie has studied this case in detail (43, p. 21), looking for correspondence between Dame Edith's script and the actual sinking, though beyond the mention of 'fire' and 'funnel' he could find no definite overlap. He points out that the words 'fear is the arch enemy' are commonly interpreted as referring to the unnecessarily large loss of life due to panic on board when the torpedo struck, but he also offers a counter suggestion. Often in the middle of automatic scripts, messages assumed to come from someone who is dead are inserted as a kind of prod or morale booster to the automatist: don't be frightened to hear this communication, don't be afraid to sound a fool, etc., and this may be the 'fear is the arch enemy' to which Dame Edith's script refers – the automatist's fear of hearing being the arch enemy of the 'dead one's' attempt to communicate.

One of Dame Edith's 'Second World War scripts', though perhaps suspiciously cryptic, does contain tantalizing phrases, including one which might possibly refer to Hitler:

> In the western fields carnage – marching – the vines on the hills, the vintage – flight – now mark this – behind the curtains of blackness there is light never doubt it – be of good cheer.
> The hand stretched out to stay Bechtesgaden – Markovitch.

This script was written in May 1915, in the midst of all the carnage of

World War I, and thus the references to 'carnage', 'fields', and 'flight' might well simply reflect Dame Edith's preoccupation with the horrors of the present rather than of some future war. Equally, 'behind the blackness there is light' might anticipate the concern which led her to become an active voice in the League of Nations. But what of 'Bechtesgaden'?

'Berchtesgaden' was the name of Adolf Hitler's mountain retreat close to the Austro-German border and it was to feature in the events leading up to World War II, but it was also a popular German tourist resort, mention of which would naturally have occurred in the press from time to time. Was Dame Edith's script simply reflecting some recent reading about Berchtesgaden, or was her hand indeed guided to foresee the retreat's later role? The latter possibility, slight as it may be, is the reason for the script's so often being cited as a possible instance of precognition.

During the Russo-Polish conflict which followed the First World War, a Polish auditory medium known as Madame Przybylska (39b) heard messages which seemed to give detailed information about future developments in the respective fortunes of the Russian and Polish armies and in the Polish political situation. Her messages were recorded during a series of private seances to friends during June and July 1920 and apparently related to events of July and August 1920.

Madame Przybylska's first message was dictated at a time when the Polish army had the upper hand on every front and the Bolsheviks were in ignominious retreat. Nevertheless she said:

> The Council of Ministers is not yet constituted, but sooner or later you will hear of Witos.
> What misfortunes! What disasters! How many dead on your battlefields! A disaster to your troops.
> During this month there will be a great change in the Council. Witos will be Prime Minister.
> A greater man than your ministers will give you help. In August everything will change. A stranger arrives, with whom Pildsudki will take counsel; he will have much influence.
> The systematic strikes will come to an end. Towards the middle of August you will see that your misfortunes change. [10 June 1920]

As it happened, the Bolsheviks began an unexpected general offensive on the war's northern front on 28 June and the Polish army was driven from Munich, Vilna and Lida. Warsaw itself was threatened, though as Madame Przybylska predicted, the city was never invaded. On 12 July she told her private audience of Warsaw society figures:

> Lenin's power grows. A flood of men invades your country, you abandon your fields. But be fearless. I bless your town; the disaster is only on the right bank of the Vistula, and all will change for the better . . . Warsaw is not on the right bank. They will not enter Warsaw.

The interesting thing about Madame Przybylska's 'messages', unlike the rather cryptic scripts of Dame Edith Lyttelton, is that they contain very specific and quite accurate detail. Not only was there the initial unexpected reverse in Poland's military fortunes, but it was indeed true that this reversal itself was to reverse in mid-August: the Poles were able to claim victory on 15 August. Further, Poland's eventual success was due largely to the intervention of a stranger named General Weygand who arrived to counsel Pildsudki, and it was also true that Mr Witos, previously a political unknown, rose to the position of Prime Minister. Other 'messages' spoken during those summer months were equally accurate in predicting battle locations and outcomes. For instance, on 12 July she said, 'Minsk, Kowel and Vilna are lost. Near Kowel many rich people are shot. Terrible news comes from the province. But in a month all will change.'

In the following weeks, Minsk, Kowel and Vilna were lost, though they were recaptured in the victory of 15 August.

Auditory Precognition
At 8.30 AM on 3 June 1964, the late Juliet, Lady Rhys Williams, an active member of the Liberal Party, Vice-President of the Economic Research Council and a former Governor of the BBC, joined her two daughters at breakfast in their Belgravia home in London. Casually, she shared with them the news that Senator Barry Goldwater had just defeated Governor Nelson Rockefeller in the California presidential election primary. She had, she said, heard about it on the radio while waking – sometime between 6.30 and 7.30.

In her own account of the radio broadcast she had heard, Lady Rhys Williams remembered the commentator saying that the voting had closed the night before, that a result could come in so quickly because this was the first fully computerized election ever to be held, and that Governor Rockefeller had conceded defeat before going home. She heard the sounds of many people in a large room as the commentator said they were 'going over to California' for a report, recognized the typical American voices in the room, and then heard the commentator explain that Senator Goldwater could not come to the microphone because he had left his campaign headquarters for a barber's shop, to have a wash and shave before going home.

There is nothing unusual about the radio broadcast which Lady Rhys Williams heard – except that the first radio broadcast to announce the Goldwater victory was on the American CBS network, which carried the news at 10.39 AM New York time (3.39 PM London time), seven hours after Lady Rhys Williams mentioned the broadcast to her daughters at breakfast. The first BBC broadcast about the election was at 5.30 PM that same afternoon, and in it, the BBC were still saying that there had as yet been no concession by Rockefeller (43, pp. 78–84).

This case is interesting not only because Lady Rhys Williams seems genuinely to have had some precognitive awareness of the election result before it was announced, but more so because she *heard* her precognitive 'vision'. The vast majority of reported cases of apparent precognition centre around some sort of precognitive visual imagery – whether in dreams or in waking visions. Auditory cases such as this are rare indeed, though not, apparently, in the life of Lady Rhys Williams.

Six months before her experience of 'hearing' the Goldwater victory broadcast, she had had a similar experience of 'pre-audition' which she reported in detail to the British SPR. This time, it was while staying at her country home in Wales that she switched on her radio at 4 AM on 17 January 1964 to hear a 'Voice of America' broadcast announcing serious racial violence in Atlanta, Georgia, as rioting broke out between members of the Ku Klux Klan and a large black crowd. Because of her own active interest in such matters, she tuned into the BBC later in the day and looked in vain in the British press for some further news about the Atlanta rioting. There was none, and she commented to both her daughter and to a neighbour how strange it seemed that such a serious incident would be mentioned only once in a single broadcast.

When Lady Rhys Williams returned to London on 26 January, she heard a BBC news broadcast about serious race riots in Atlanta, but this time there were follow-up reports in both the British and American press. Curious now as to whether there had indeed been rioting reported on the morning of 17 January, Lady Rhys Williams wrote to the 'Voice of America' in Washington to enquire about any earlier broadcasts. They confirmed that there had been an earlier outbreak of rioting, on 20 January, and that the first intimation of the trouble to come had been a disturbance in Atlanta on the evening of 18 January, when the police had had to be called out. The 'Voice of America' had broadcast this earlier trouble, but some 48 hours after Lady Rhys Williams first 'heard' their news flash (31).

Precognitive Gambling

The case of John Godley, now Lord Kilbracken, discussed in the last chapter is the best on record of someone's successfully dreaming the results of horse races before the races have been run. There are many other reported instances of someone's backing a certain horse or a certain number because he has had a 'hunch' just before making his bet (and while fully awake), but the following case seems to have other and more definite features which make it interesting. It is both a good case of apparent waking precognition and, because of the particular way in which the bulk of the gambler's precognitive 'flashes', as she calls them, occurred, it is particularly relevant to later attempts (Chapter Twelve) to apply quantum mechanical models to the problem of precognition.

This case has not been previously reported, and though the gambler concerned would be willing to co-operate in any attempts to corroborate her experiences, their nature would for the most part make this difficult. Whether her winnings were obtained in the way she describes depends on her own judgement and honesty. She is a member of the SPR, now, but she says that she had no interest in psychic phenomena before her own strange gambling experiences began. She has written the following report, signing it only 'Miss H. R.':

> I got my first 'flash' in 1973, just before the Grand National. I knew nothing about horse racing and had never been inside a betting shop, but all the national fuss about this race (Miss H. R. is a Canadian) made me want to participate. I looked at the list of runners posted on the betting shop wall and 'Red Rum' just jumped out at me. I backed him at 15/1 and, of course, won. It was Red Rum's first Grand National win, and he was not the favourite that year.
>
> The next year I backed Red Rum in the National, but that was a case of judgement. However, in 1975, 1976 and 1977, I had the same experience of a horse's name (twice that of a relative outsider) just 'jumping out' at me as I looked at the names in the betting shop. In those years I won on L'Escargot, Rag Trade and Red Rum. I still knew nothing about 'form', and took no interest in racing apart from the Grand National.

I was first taken to a casino by a friend three years ago. I had never been to one before and knew nothing about casino games, but I was fascinated by the roulette wheel and decided to try my luck at that. I had only £3 with me, and by betting on red or black, I slowly increased that to £23 before stopping. I put this increase in my fortunes down to 'beginner's luck' and thought no more about it for several months.

It was when I had lost my job and was desperately short of money that I revisited the casino and first noticed the phenomenon that was to repeat itself from then on whenever I needed money very badly for some authentic purpose – such as paying my rent, or some bill. I noticed that I would get a strong 'feeling' about a given number from time to time, and that this number would then come up.

I have played roulette off and on many times since first noticing those 'feelings' for numbers, and have been able to see the pattern of them. What actually happens when I get the 'feeling' is that my attention is suddenly drawn to a number on the roulette cloth, not on the wheel. I just find that my eyes have fixed on it. When this happens, it is almost always in that split second just before the croupier calls 'No more bets,' though on occasion my attention is solicited just after the ball has been spun. I have never experienced a flash of vision before the ball has left the croupier's hand.

These precognitive flashes do not of course happen every time the roulette wheel is spun, but they do happen frequently enough to ensure that I nearly always come out well ahead after a session's play. Occasionally the flash is a 'near miss' instead of a direct hit – i.e., my attention is drawn to a number on the table, but in fact it is the adjacent number which actually comes up.

Two other aspects of my roulette experiences may be relevant. When having these flashes, my concentration is so great that I am almost in a kind of trance and oblivious to my surroundings. I become both mentally and physically exhausted after an hour of such concentration, and need a full day to recover the normal concentration of my brain. The other thing is that if I become greedy, trying to win more money than I actually need, or go to the casino simply as an entertainment, I do not get the flashes and have the same luck as any other player at the table.

As will be seen in later discussions about the mechanics of precognition, both in its possible relation to quantum phenomena and in relation to attempts to investigate it under laboratory conditions, the most interesting aspects of Miss H. R.'s roulette experiences are:

1.   the fact that she gets her flashes within a split second of the roulette ball's actually falling into a position on the wheel;

2   that she occasionally experiences a 'near miss' with her flash instead of the number she has been drawn to; and

3   that she requires exhausting concentration of a deeper than normal kind to experience her flashes.

Her inability to win money which she did not actually require to meet pressing need is within the tradition of the occult that psychic ability is a gift which would be misused were it turned to mere profit. This same tradition is borne out in another reported case of 'psychic gambling'.

In his collection of visions and premonitions, Goethe's friend Johann Jung-Stilling, a physician, professor and believer in the supernatural, recounted the story of a Berlin apothecary, Dr Christopher Knape. As a young apprentice, Knape accurately dreamt the winning number of the state lottery and thus came into a small sum of money. A few years later he dreamt of lottery numbers again, but as he could only recall the first two of the five digits with any certainty, he gambled very cautiously and managed to win only the equivalent of twenty dollars. But the following year he dreamt of the winning number with such clarity that he decided to risk everything he had by investing heavily – only to find that he was given his investment money back because all the tickets bearing that number were already sold. That number did win the lottery, but Dr Knape had gained nothing by his dream (32, p. 135).

4   Experimental Studies of Precognition

Most of the cases of foresight or precognition discussed so far, like most instances of ESP in general, were spontaneous; they just happened. Quite without inducement or warning, and often with very unsettling effect, seemingly ordinary people in the natural course of their everyday lives apparently experience from time to time previsions of future events, telepathic communications, sounds of things that go 'bump in the night', and various other even stranger happenings that make up the body of things called psychic phenomena.

The advantages of studying the spontaneous cases of ESP are that there are so many of them and, more often than not, the ones that get reported 'make a good read'. The disadvantages are that spontaneous cases are unpredictable, uncontrolled (and thus open to many interpretations), and all too often unbelievable – sometimes even to the people who have experienced them.

Towards the end of the last century, it became clear to serious-minded investigators that if such phenomena were ever to be understood, or even verified, they would have to be observed under controlled, experimental conditions. It was towards this end that the Society for Psychical Research was founded in 1882, its founders' aim being to turn the dispassionate spotlight of rigorous scientific method on to the heretofore murky waters of psychical phenomena. Their successors have succeeded to the point that parapsychology is now almost more scientific than science itself. Computers, statistical tables and laboratory technicians who patiently repeat quite dull experiments thousands of times have replaced the colourful world of mediums and fortune-tellers. While physicist colleagues in adjacent laboratories enjoy the Alice in Wonderland pleasures of unbridled speculation about the seemingly endless proliferation of possibly forever undetectable sub-atomic particles, in the parapsychology laboratory it is almost as if an experiment that is interesting must be invalid. Boredom, perversely, has become a measuring stick of success in experimental parapsychology.

But the experimental side of parapsychology – the attempt to induce psychic phenomena in the laboratory upon demand, and under controlled conditions – is only one branch of the past century's research efforts. Outside the laboratory, many SPR members have seen their task as diligently recording and scrupulously investigating those spontaneous phenomena which come their way. Thus volunteers from the Society have often sat for nights in some allegedly haunted house waiting for its resident apparition to put in an appearance, or patiently interviewed anybody to whom a percipient dreamer may have related the details of an apparently precognitive dream before its farseeing contents were fulfilled.

Ironically perhaps, the first really systematic experimental study of precognition ever undertaken was done by someone who was not affiliated with the Society for Psychical Research, who indeed was said to enjoy only a 'cool and unfruitful' relationship with the Society even at the best of times. He was J. W. Dunne, whose now classic *An Experiment With Time* (15) could justifiably be said to have 'put precognition on the map.'

J. W. Dunne's 'Time Displacement'

Dunne, an aeronautics engineer born in 1875, was a man almost at war with Time, at least with our conventional notion of it. He devoted much of his life to the project, not entirely unsuccessful, of proving that precognition is a fact and one to be reckoned with. 'If prevision be a fact,' he wrote, 'it is a fact which destroys absolutely the entire basis of all our past assumptions of the universe.'

Though Dunne's experimental study of precognition consisted solely of meticulously recording his own dreams and then measuring their contents against coming events, *An Experiment With Time*, published in 1927, was really the first studied attempt to treat precognition as a serious issue. He used precognition as proof against a view of time which he knew (being aware of at least the wider implications of Einstein's work) was needlessly constrictive and outmoded, and he wrote about it in a way that could fire the imaginations of people who couldn't possibly arrive at a new view of Time via the then almost incomprehensible path of Einstein's equations.

Dunne proposed his own Theory of Serial Time which took as its starting point the obvious feature of reflexive self-awareness: if X is being conscious of the words printed on the pages of a book there is also an aspect of X, which is conscious of his being conscious of those words, and so on. Dunne suggests the same thing for the structure of Time.

In his Theory of Serial Time, he proposes that there are several Time dimensions, akin to the several layers of potential self-awareness, so that an event taking place in Time dimension A could in turn be seen in perspective from Time dimension B, which in turn could be seen in further perspective from Time dimension C, and so on in infinite regress back to some Absolute Time from which the whole universe is laid out in a God's eye view. Further, Dunne suggests that while our waking life takes place in Time dimension A, when we are asleep and dreaming we are given access to the higher Time dimensions. Thus, while dreaming, it should be perfectly natural that an event which would seem not yet to have happened from the perspective of Time dimension A would be easily visible to the level of consciousness observing it from Time dimension B. On waking, we would think that we had perceived a 'future event', because it does indeed lie in the 'future' with respect to our limited, waking Time dimension.

In itself, Dunne's theory of Serial Time is universally rejected as somewhat woolly-minded metaphysical speculation. It has no basis whatever in science, and as a theory of how precognition works it suffers the additional weakness that it could only hope to deal with precognitive dreams and not with the full range of reported cases. None the less, *An Experiment With Time* will always have a place on the bookshelves of psychic researchers for the issues it raises and for its diligent cataloguing of Dunne's for the most part rather mundane (and perhaps, therefore, more credible) precognitive dreams.

Dunne's method was, in principle, very simple. Apparently taking to heart Frank Podmore's uneasiness about using dream material as evidence for any precognitive ability because 'the elusive impressions' of our dreams are so quickly forgotten, or only half-remembered and then later embellished to accord with waking reality, Dunne recommended that his readers sleep with a pad and pencil under their pillows. Then, 'immediately on waking, before you even open your eyes, you set yourself to remember the rapidly vanishing dream.' Unfortunately for both Dunne and his work, he failed to take the equally simple precaution of having his dream notebooks witnessed each day by someone else, thus losing the confidence of the Society for Psychical Research, which requires such witnessing as a standard practice.

Dunne, however, described at length many of the dreams which he so meticulously recorded, and put these descriptions together with their seemingly positive follow-ups. In 1901, for example, invalided out of the Boer War and resting in a spot near Khartoum, he dreamed of three white men in faded khaki arriving from South Africa, apparently by foot. Thinking it odd that anyone should walk so far, he questioned them, and one said, 'We have come right through from the Cape [trekking on foot]'. The next day, over breakfast, he read the following headlines in his newspaper: 'The Cape to Cairo, 'Daily Telegraph' Expedition in Khartoum – the *Daily Telegraph* expedition arrived at Khartoum after a magnificent journey, etc., etc.'

In 1902, encamped with the 6th Mounted Infantry in South Africa's Orange Free State, Dunne dreamed of an island in imminent danger from an erupting volcano. He pictured the little fissures developing in the volcano's sides, the jets of steam gushing out of them; and he 'knew' that it was an island under French domination – and that if the authorities did not act quickly to evacuate the natives, 4,000 lives could be lost. A few days later, when his regiment received their batch of newspapers, he read, 'Volcano Disaster in Martinique, Town Swept Away, An Avalanche of Flame, Probable Loss of Life Over 40,000 Lives.' (He got his 4,000 wrong by dropping a zero; but he insisted he had misread the newspaper report and for a long time thought it *had* said 4,000 instead of 40,000.)

Others of Dunne's dreams were more trivial. He dreamed of a combination lock, and then the next day read of such a lock in a book; he dreamed of a pile of coins resting on a book and the next day saw just such a pile of coins (sixpences) in that position; he dreamed of a shower of sparks flying in his face from (he presumed) a swarm of cigarette ends and the next day, while he was using the bellows on a fire, a shower of sparks flew into his face – and so on.

When Dunne first realized that he was dreaming glimpses of the future before it happened, it disturbed him. 'No one,' he said, 'could derive any considerable pleasure from the supposition that he is a freak.' He seriously entertained the notion that he must bear some mental abnormality:

> I was suffering, seemingly, from some extraordinary fault in my relation to reality, something so uniquely wrong that it compelled me to perceive, at rare intervals, large blocks of otherwise perfectly normal personal experience displaced from their proper positions in Time. That such things could occur at all was a most interesting piece of knowledge. But, unfortunately, in the circumstances it could be knowledge to only one person – myself.

Though, as we shall see, viewing a faculty such as precognitive ability as a mental aberration is one explanation put forward by some psychologists who have encountered it, Dunne himself soon gave up the notion that he was abnormal. J. B. Priestley agreed: in his *Man And Time*, he described Dunne as being, 'as far removed from any suggestion of the seer, the sage, the crank and crackpot, as it is possible to imagine . . . He belonged to the military section of Britain's old upper class, and had its staccato and not highly articulate manner in talk; he looked and behaved like the old regular officer-type crossed with a mathematician and engineer.'

With great relief, Dunne soon discovered that other people spoke of having precognitive dreams, and in time he came to believe that everybody experiences them, whether they are aware of it or not. All dreams, he concluded, are a blending of images from the past and images from the future, and some foreknowledge about the future is thus a standard part of our mental makeup.

Beyond the role his book has played in making precognition acceptable to a wider public than it might otherwise have been, Dunne's work is important in another respect. His catalogue of dreams provided detailed written material which made it possible to some extent to analyse the nature of their precognitive content. In doing so, he noticed that his previsions often focused on such things as pages of books or newspaper headlines. This raised the possibility that what he was seeing in advance was not actual future events but his own future perceptions of those events. Such a possibility figures prominently in the various attempts to put forward a physical theory of how precognition might work.

The pity about Dunne's otherwise fine work was the failure to have his dream accounts witnessed, and thus the failure to put them beyond all suspicion. In 1933, the Society for Psychical Research tried to repeat Dunne's experiment under proper (witnessed) conditions. In all 430 dreams were collected and recorded, but the result of comparing them with any real events that might then have happened was very poor – there simply was no noticeable correspondence between recorded dream materials and waking events.

Sargent & Harley Laboratory Experiments
Very recently (1981), however, Cambridge University researchers did carry out a variation on Dunne's dream experiments with apparent success. Working at the Psychological Laboratory, Dr Carl Sargent

(Cambridge's first ever Ph.D. in parapsychology) and colleague, Trevor Harley, did a run of 44 laboratory trials to test for precognition in their subjects – 20 were trials on dreaming subjects and 24 on subjects subjected to a form of mild sensory deprivation called the Ganzfeld state (29).

In the Ganzfeld, all normal sensory channels associated with ordinary thinking are blocked. While the research subject relaxes in a reclining chair, his eyes are covered with half ping pong balls which allow a uniform white haze to affect the retina, while his ears are covered with headphones through which 'white noise' is transmitted. White noise (a combination of all auditory frequencies) sounds like gently sizzling bacon and tends to scatter organized thoughts.

In the case of the dream trials, the Cambridge team's method was to ask a selection of research subjects to make written records of their dreams immediately upon waking. The dream transcripts were then 'matched' by a researcher for any likeness to one of four possible pictures printed on a set of cards. (In all there were 200 cards, 50 of each picture.) Likenesses between dream transcripts and cards were ranked in order of preference according to which card picture best corresponded to the dream contents, and these rankings were recorded.

The *following* day, after the matching had been done and ranked, a card was selected randomly (using random number tables) from the pack of 200 by machine, and Sargent and Harley then compared the card chosen to the previous day's ranked correlations between dream imagery and card imagery. The chance expectation of there being any correlation between a dreamt image and the picture on the top-ranked card, since there were four different pictures, would be 1 time in 4 (25%). But in fact, Sargent & Harley found a much higher correlation. 40% of their dreaming subjects dreamed something like the following day's card picture (and 41.7% of their sensory deprivation subjects did so).

The Experiments of J. B. Rhine

In both method and content, the laboratory-oriented Cambridge work in the 1980s, so very different from Dunne's 'home study' approach, was anticipated by the pioneering work of J. B. Rhine half a century earlier. It was Rhine who was responsible for creating almost single-handedly the whole new science of parapsychology. After he founded the first officially funded academic research unit in 1932, his

'Parapsychological Laboratory' at Duke University, experimental parapsychology became a significant research industry.

Though debate as to the worthiness of the enterprise and controversy about the actual meaning of its results still rages both within and outside psychical research circles, several score of universities around the world now incorporate ESP research programmes; professional and semi-professional journals in the subject proliferate; and even governments have got into the act. Both America and the Soviet Union seem prepared to include parapsychology in the arsenal of potential weapons each is stockpiling in the Great Arms Race.

J. B. Rhine's original research efforts at Duke University were directed towards devising laboratory tests aimed at proving once and for all the existence of telepathy,* and in this he was remarkably successful. He evolved a programme of card-guessing experiments in which a subject was asked to guess telepathically which of five possible designs on cards had just been dealt by a laboratory technician, and the results his subjects achieved were well above chance expectation. Ironically, it was in direct response to these telepathy experiments that the first really methodical study of precognition ever carried out under laboratory conditions came about – as an accident.

The Soal–Shackleton Experiments

In 1934, S. G. Soal, a mathematics lecturer at Queen Mary College, London and a member of the Council of the Society for Psychical Research (later its President) had hoped to duplicate the impressive telepathic card-guessing results produced by Rhine and his colleagues at Duke. He inserted an advertisement in various London papers asking for subjects to come forward, and offered a financial reward to any who could guess correctly 12 out of 25 cards.

Soal's cards, like those used by Rhine, were Zener cards bearing the symbols of circles, squares, plus-signs, wavy lines and stars. Each pack of 25 cards contained 5 cards bearing each symbol and, according to chance expectation, a person should be able to guess correctly 20% of the time – that is, should be able to name 5 cards correctly from the pack of 25. The odds against the subject's fulfilling Soal's requirement to guess correctly 12 out of the 25 cards are *thousands to one*.

*In fact, Rhine seldom referred to telepathy as such, preferring the more general term ESP to keep open the possibility that any given 'hit' might just as well be an instance of clairvoyance or psychokinesis rather as necessarily telepathy.

In the experiment, the subject sat on one side of an opaque screen, while Dr Soal sat on the other, turning up the cards one by one as they appeared through an automatic shuffling process. Again like Rhine, Soal meticulously recorded the subject's guesses and compared them with the results that should have been delivered up by chance.

Unlike Rhine, however, Soal appeared to have absolutely no success in demonstrating the existence of telepathy. Four years, 160 subjects and 128,350 separate guesses produced no more than the expected chance results. He communicated his disappointment to Rhine, whose wife Louisa commented, 'He was about to conclude either that reports from the United States were phoney or else that Englishmen do not have ESP.'

Soal's friend and fellow ESP researcher Whately Carington had a different possible explanation to put forward. In his own experiments with telepathy, Carington had noted a 'time-displacement' in his subjects' guesses and thought the same might have happened in Soal's data. He suggested that Soal re-analyse his results, looking this time not for direct hits, but for guesses that scored correctly against the *next* card to be dealt. Such analysis produced an altogether different picture. Especially with one particular subject, the photographer Basil Shackleton, the new way of looking at things produced results so striking that the odds against it having happened by chance were billions to one. Without intending to, Soal had, apparently, produced devastating experimental evidence for precognition: for while Shackleton had shown a distressingly dismal incapacity telepathically to guessing which card had in fact just been turned up, he had appeared to demonstrate a remarkable genius for precognitively guessing the card that was *about* to be turned up. Neither Soal nor any of his assistants could have known this card in advance, because the pack of cards had been shuffled randomly by machine, and thus the order in which the cards lay was 'known' only to that machine.

Soal was so impressed by the results of the reinterpretation of his data that he set out on a new, and very lengthy, series of card-guessing experiments with Shackleton, this time knowing that he was looking for evidence of precognition rather than telepathy. He was assisted by his colleague Mrs K. M. Goldney and by many respected scientists from the British Society for Psychical Research; and the results of the new tests were the same, with Shackleton seeming to demonstrate precognitive capacities beyond anything that could be explained by chance. In consequence, it was realized, the 'bogey man' of ESP research would have to be investigated seriously – however little those who conducted such research liked the idea. As Rhine put it, 'Precognition simply cannot be physical in any present-day sense of the word! Indeed the sheer contrariness it presents to the causal sequence in which we usually see things happen in nature makes it, at one and the same time, both a scientific prize and a scientific outlaw.' (62, p. 73). But intrigued by this 'scientific outlaw', and aware of its outstanding implications, Rhine had to set about testing for it with all the assiduousness and scientific rigour his research team could bring to bear.

As objections were raised to any given method of administering the tests, the method was altered. Human card shufflers gave way to machines, and mathematical random number tables were used to generate purely chance sequences for the positioning of cards in the pack. But no matter what refinements were added, in Rhine's laboratory as well as in several others in America and Britain, subjects' precognitive guesses continued to score successfully well above chance. By 1948, Rhine concluded that, after all, if telepathy were possible (as he believed without a shadow of doubt it was), then it followed that the possibility of precognition was not so unexpected:

> The evidence we had obtained by the autumn of 1933, concerning the relation of extra-sensory perception to the physical world, made the ESP of future events a reasonable, if not a logically necessary, corollary. The conception that the mind might transcend time limitations followed as a natural consequence of the distance tests with ESP. For if ESP was space-free, it must also be time-free within our space-time universe of physics. Time is a function of spatial change – that is, physical movement in space requires time; hence to be out of space is to be out of time as well. Perception of past or future events was therefore in line with the perception of distant happenings [62, p. 60]

But there is a strange irony in Rhine's conversion, brought about as it was through work done in response to Soal's apparently impressive experiments with Basil Shackleton. For in the late 1970s, new evidence came to light which suggested that the last of the Soal–Shackleton results might well have been faked (46). Without question, the new evidence established that at the very least Soal had manipulated his experimental data to make Shackleton's performance appear more definitive than it had actually been.

The controversy surrounding this discovery continues, and it may never be settled once and for all whether Shackleton had no ESP ability whatever and thus the whole experiment was a lie, or whether

Soal simply 'dressed up' his data to present an even, consistent picture where in fact Shackleton – a moody and unpredictable man – had been erratic in his ESP performance. Whichever interpretation one takes, however, Soal's work will remain under a permanent shadow, and yet it was this perhaps fraudulent effort which inspired the much more credible work subsequently done by Rhine and others.

There are in fact scores of other precognition research projects that might be cited, most using some variation on the card-guessing theme. Such experimental work is self-generating in a sense as, the more evidence that is adduced for precognition, the more scientists and psychologists feel impelled to subject it to laboratory scrutiny. But there are three instances of research which are especially interesting, both because they depart from the standard card-guessing format and because they may help to shed some light on how precognition, if it exists, might actually work.

The Stanford Experiments
In a radical departure from card-guessing work, two Stanford Research Institute physicists, Russell Targ and Harold Puthoff, have produced some very impressive results with research into precognitive viewing of real life situations.

Between 1976 and 1977, Targ and Puthoff (73, pp. 73–9) conducted four experiments involving a precognitively gifted subject (Hella Hammid) who remained inside the laboratory while fellow researchers were dispatched to previously unknown destinations by motor car. The object of the experiments was to see whether the laboratory subject could describe, in advance, visual details of the place which the travelling research assistants would then visit.

As part of the built-in 'controls' for the Targ–Puthoff experiments, the travelling research assistants had no idea in advance to what destination they would be travelling. The object of keeping them in ignorance was to exclude any possibility of telepathy between them and the laboratory subject. Instead, the research assistants left the laboratory carrying ten sealed envelopes, each enclosing detailed instructions to travel to some different destination. The envelopes had been selected from a much larger stock by use of random number generators.

Fifteen minutes before the travelling researchers were to open one of their ten envelopes (which one to open also being determined by a random number generator), the laboratory subject was asked to describe or draw any visual details she could 'pick up' from the places the researchers were about to visit. Thirty minutes after she had made these guesses, and only fifteen minutes after learning their destinations themselves, the researchers arrived at some one of the pre-chosen spots.

Later, scientists who had no previous relationship with the experiment were asked to match up the laboratory subject's precognitive descriptions with photographic details of the actual locations visited. The detailed correspondence between the precognitive descriptions and the actual sites (the Palo Alto Yacht Harbour, Stanford University Hospital Garden, a children's swing and play area, and Palo Alto City Hall) was well beyond anything which could be explained away by chance or 'coincidence', and seemed to satisfy the rigorous criteria of those involved that genuine precognition had been at work.

The same type of precognitive research as that designed by Targ and Puthoff has since been carried out at Mundelein College in Chicago by a team of psychologists, with similarly apparently successful results, though Professor John Taylor (76, pp. 78–9) has raised some doubt about the significance of these remote-viewing tests on the grounds that the matching up by a third party of a given location and the subject's description of it, in itself involves a high degree of subjective judgement. This same criticism was made by two New Zealand researchers, D. Marks and R. Kammann, in a letter to *Nature* questioning certain of the Stanford experiments* and presenting what they felt to be evidence that in at least one of these the research subject had provided extraneous cues which helped the third parties to match his descriptions with the target sites (45, pp. 680–81).

In reply to this criticism, Targ and Puthoff, and their colleague Charles Tart, edited the transcripts in question to remove all the potential cues mentioned by Marks and Kammann in their letter. They then submitted the whole edited series to a new independent judge who still succeeded in matching up 7 out of 10 'distant viewing' descriptions with their actual locations. This lead the Stanford team to conclude:

> . . . On the basis of an independently conducted empirical test, we reject as invalid the Marks–Kammann conjecture that success in the first-published study on remote viewing is to be attributed to cueing artefacts rather than to transcript/target correlations. [74, p. 191]

*A different series of experiments than those conducted with Hella Hammid; the subject in this case was Patrick Price.

Texas Quantum-Level Experiments

In perhaps the most interesting and promising variation on the card-guessing technique so far devised for precognition research, physicist Dr Helmut Schmidt – who served as Director of Rhine's laboratory at Duke in 1970 and now works at the Mind Science Foundation in San Antonio, Texas – has carried out a series of experiments involving lights triggered by sub-atomic processes (65). Because his technique does use quantum level events generated by the random decay process of radioactive atoms, it is by far the most important piece of research available for purposes of attempts to explain how precognition works.

Schmidt's work involved designing a new electronic apparatus, a box with four lights connected to on/off switches. These switches were connected to a random number generator which could decide arbitrarily whether to switch on light 1, 2, 3 or 4, and the random number generator itself was connected by complex circuitry to the ionizing radiation given off by a sample of decaying strontium-90. Thus the only control over which of the four lights on Schmidt's box would next light up was the strontium-90's completely random radioactive decay process. His experiment consisted of asking a research subject to guess which light would come on next, and to register his guess by pushing the button which was attached to that light.

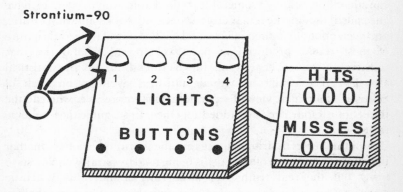

In Helmut Schmidt's experiments, the unpredictable radioactive decay process of strontium-90 is used to generate a random signal which will arbitrarily switch on one of the four lights. The precognitive research subject is asked to guess which will light up next by pushing one of the four associated buttons, and his success or failure is registered on the counter at right.

The results of Schmidt's experiment look like, and are taken by many parapsychologists to be, conclusive proof that some people can indeed see an even before it happens.* In 7,600 trials with one subject, a fellow physicist, the subject guessed correctly which light would next light up 37.7% of the time, (the odds against chance of such a result would be 10 billion to 1) where by chance expectation he should only have guessed correctly 25% of the time (because there were four lights). But when the experiment was enlarged to include three subjects guessing 63,000 times, their level of success dropped to 26.1% – slightly above chance, but not much. And in another set of experiments, where three subjects guessed a total of 20,000 times made up of four series of trials, their success rate above chance was only 0.25%. So what is happening here? Do we conclude that Schmidt's seemingly impressive results in fact come to nothing on closer scrutiny? Looking at this question sheds some light on what to make of a whole body of results obtained in experimental parapsychology and also highlights one reason why the whole field is still so controversial, despite all its scientific trappings.

In the last experiment just discussed, in which Schmidt had his subjects guessing which light would come on next a total of 20,000 times, the experiment was in fact broken down into four separate trial runs of 5,000 guesses each. In two of these trials, his subjects guessed correctly at a rate significantly above chance, and in the other two they guessed significantly *below* chance expectation. So in each of the trials considered separately, something remarkable would seem to have happened, though the remarkable happenings were somewhat erratic, and even opposite in their effect – and it is because of the erratic nature of most results produced in parapsychological laboratories that researchers rely so heavily on the pictures built up by statistical averages. Yet, while individual statistical averages on each of Schmidt's four runs, viewed separately, look impressive, when all the results of all four runs are added together, this significance tends to melt away.

And this brings us straight up against the thorny question of whether the all-important tool of statistics is being used by parapsychologists to bring out the real truth over large runs of individually erratic experimental trials (as adherents of experimental parapsychology would claim), or whether in fact statistical averages are being

Schmidt himself prefers to see his results as proof that psychokinesis underlies so-called precognition (see p. 293).

manipulated (perhaps unintentionally) in a way that makes insignificant results appear significant.

The Oxford mathematician G. Spencer Brown has in fact written at length (85, pp. 73–9) on this question, arguing that in his view the 'statistically significant' data of psychical research are not significant of anything other than as a general pointer towards where researchers might look further. He feels that parapsychological experiments intended to study extrasensory communication 'have in most cases degenerated into experiments in pure probability', and he devotes a great deal of analysis to the flaws of reasoning which lie behind such notions as randomness and statistical averages.

Behind the seemingly significant guise of 'meaningful statistical averages' such as those produced by Schmidt, Brown points out, there are always only the constant streams of erratic *new* phenomena – never (with very rare exceptions) are there any genuinely *repeatable* results, which are one standard criterion for any good scientific experiment.

It could of course be argued that the whole standard of repeatability, and a good many other of the experimental parameters so crucial to mainstream science, are inappropriate to the phenomena with which the parapsychologist must deal, but in that case it might be best if more experimental parapsychologists were themselves to admit this (as a few have). Such an open admission – though it would spark further controversy – would at least put paid to the rather common charge of sceptics who argue that experimental parapsychology is deliberately steeped in 'pseudo-scientific obfuscation.'

Charting the Time Factor in Precognition

In research of a very different sort, devoted to studying rather than demonstrating precognition, a British clinical psychologist, J. E. Orme of the Sheffield Area Psychological Service, undertook the task of compiling a survey of 148 separate cases of spontaneous precognition. He hoped that from so large a number of cases, some general tendencies and trends might be noticeable.

Orme's research (54) does highlight many trends which are useful for classifying precognitive experiences according to the content of the experience or the state (i.e., dreaming, trance, waking vision, etc.) of the percipient; but the major thrust of his survey was to measure the time factor in precognitive phenomena – the amount of time which lapsed between the precognitive vision and the actual happening of the event foreseen. His results make up one of the most solid contributions yet towards offering a basis for understanding the actual mechanics of precognition.

Orme drew his examples of precognition from four sources, all classics in the field: he took 48 from the experiences described by Dunne in his *An Experiment With Time*, 41 from Barker's study of the Aberfan disaster, 30 from E. Lyttelton's *Some Cases Of Prediction*, and 29 from H. F. Saltmarsh's *Foreknowledge*. All but the Dunne experiences were verified by corroborative evidence from witnesses, and Dunne's accounts are generally regarded as honest, if for no other reason that that they are so trivial – if he were going to invent precognitive experiences, the argument goes, surely he would have invented some more interesting ones!

Of the 148 experiences studied by Orme, 57 (38.5%) happened within 24 hours of the foreseen event, 14 (9.5%) within the next 24 hours, and the rest fell off progressively as the distance in time between prevision and event lengthened. All but 42 took place within a

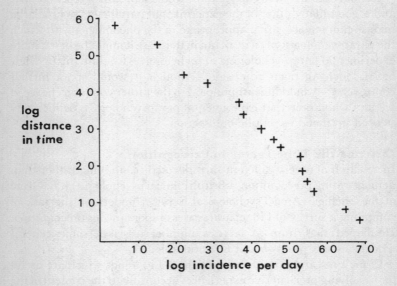

Orme charted the time-factor in 148 cases of spontaneous precognition and the results are dramatically illustrated in compressed form in this log curve which shows that the greatest number of precognitions occurred within a very short time interval before the foreseen event. With longer time spans before the actual event, there were fewer and fewer reported precognitions. (Curve reprinted from *Journal of the Society of Psychical Research*, Vol. 47, No. 760.)

fortnight of the event, and only 7 showed a time interval of more than a year.

In Orme's study, both dreaming and waking precognitive experiences were time-dependent, but the waking ones apparently more so. This corroborates reports from two other sources. In his *The Roots of Coincidence* (38), Arthur Koestler mentions that in Shoal's card-guessing experiments with Basil Shackleton, Shackleton's predictions (if they were not *all* faked) were most accurate if the time interval between guesses was 2.6 seconds. If the rate of turning up the cards was doubled, giving a time interval of only 1.4 seconds, Shackleton then showed a tendency to guess which card would turn up after the next *two* turns. This result implies a constancy, or optimum period of time lapse between prevision and event, which does not necessarily accord with the thesis that precognitions are more frequent over shorter time intervals, but given the suspect nature of Soal's data it's not possible to know whether this constancy was real or invented in Shackleton's case.

It was also true that in the example of the roulette predictions of Miss H. R., she reported that her 'flashes' of prevision always happened in the very brief time interval between the ball's leaving the croupier's hand and its landing in a given slot, 'usually in that split second just before the croupier calls "no more bets".' Thus her case, if valid, would further support Orme's conclusion that 'precognition refers to events near in time rather than more distant ones.'

Whether Orme's further assertion that, 'the close nature of the relationship between the incidence and distance in time might well suggest that this characteristic indicates something fundamental about the nature of precognition,' is also true may be better judged after looking at possible links between precognitive events and sub-atomic events as described by quantum physics (see Chapter Twelve).

PART TWO

Who Has Precognition?

5 Precognition in Animals

Early on in his classic study of meaningful coincidence, Jung relates the evocative story of a patient's death apparently being foretold by a flock of birds (37, p. 31).

Suspecting his patient of displaying mild heart symptoms, Jung had arranged for him to be examined by a specialist. Shortly after the man left home to keep this appointment, his wife noticed with alarm that a large flock of birds descended on their house. For her, the birds' arrival seemed portentous because at the deaths of both her mother and her grandmother, similar flocks of birds had taken up a vigil outside the death chamber. A few hours later, though the specialist had just given him a clean bill of health, the man collapsed in the street and was brought home dying.

Such stories are not uncommon. An American psychoanalyst relates a similar incident regarding his gardener. While the two were speaking one afternoon about the gardener's mother, a robin fell from the sky, crashed on to the bonnet of a van and fell dead at their feet. The gardener saw this as an omen and rushed home, only to arrive just as his mother was dying (41, p. 200).

Writing very soon after the founding of the Society for Psychical Research, Frank Podmore relates the story of a doctor's daughter who saw 'a strange, slim, graceful looking little bird, with a very tiny head, rather blueish grey' every day for several days prior to a death in the family. During these visits, the bird tapped the window of the family house and dirtied the window glass with its feet. After the death, the bird kept up its visits until the funeral, and then never came again (58, p. 344).

Plutarch tells us that the day before the death of Caesar, 'solitary specimens of birds began flying down into the forum,' and Suetonius paints an even more graphic image with his report that, 'A little bird called the King Bird, flew into the Hall of Pompey with a sprig of laurel in its beak – pursued by a swarm of different birds from a nearby copse, which tore it to pieces there and then.' And Ovid, describing the same event, claims that, 'In a thousand places the Stygian screech owl gave its ominous warning and dogs howled by night.'

Similarly, there is at least one anecdotal account that just before the death of Abraham Lincoln, the President's dog began racing around the White House 'in a frenzy, and kept up a dirge of unholy howling,' (66, p. 86) and anthropologists working among Australian Aborigines report that these tribesmen often claim that their first knowledge of a relative's death comes from seeing a bird or animal which was the dead man's guiding spirit (totem).

Indeed, throughout the literature some of the most graphic and seemingly impressive accounts of alleged precognitive and other ESP abilities relate to the behaviour of mammals, birds and insects, and the widely held view that such creatures are often gifted with 'second sight' is as old as the history of our race. In the myths and legends of primitive man, as well as in the fairy tales of our own childhood, this animal gift is often credited with assisting or even wholly explaining the prophetic powers of our human seers.

In the Celtic legend of Conn-eda, the mythical hero king of Ireland, Conn-eda must make a dangerous, and seemingly impossible, journey into the Fairy Realm to capture three golden apples, a black steed and a hound which belong to the Fairy King. He turns to a great Druid for advice, but the Druid admits that even he hasn't enough power to help Conn-eda with such a task. There is, however, he says, 'a certain Bird of the Human Head, concealed in a wilderness. This strange creature is famous for its knowledge of past, present and future.' Conn-eda seeks out the bird which, speaking 'in a croaking human voice,' tells him all he needs to know and foretells his success.

According to Herodotus, birds were frequently associated with oracles. He relates that one version of the story of how the oracles of Dodona in Greece and of Ammon in Libya were founded is that two black doves flew away from the temple at Thebes in Egypt: one came to Dodona, perched on an oak and then, speaking in a human voice, told the people that there it was intended there should be an oracle of Zeus; the other dove flew to Libya and similarly instructed the Libyans.

Amongst the Paleolithic and Neolithic tribes of Asia, Indonesia, and North America (and still today where certain isolated remnants of these earlier cultures survive), the belief in animal foresight was firmly embodied in the rituals and traditions of the creature-oriented shamanistic religions. The shaman – the tribal medicine man – could cure disease, bring the rain, guide the hunt or prophesy coming events, but he often relied for such magic powers on communication with a guiding animal spirit.

Each shaman would have an animal-mother or origin-animal (elk, tiger, bear, etc.) which embodied his prophetic gift, or a bird or animal 'familiar' to assist him. After working himself into the ecstatic trance that would allow him to leave his body behind, the shaman's spirit could travel freely throughout the universe making contact with other spirits, the animal helpers whose visionary powers enabled him to penetrate both the past and the future.

One group of present day 'shamans' in modern China – the seismologists – no longer leave their bodies behind when wanting to glimpse the future; but they do foresake their technical instruments for the more advanced foreknowledge of impending earthquakes to be gained from observing the erratic behaviour of many birds, animals and insects, hours – often days – before any earth tremor registers on even the most sensitive seismograph.

The Chinese suffer the highest annual average of serious earth tremors (6, or higher, on the Richter scale) of any country in the world; yet they have had more success than any other nation in markedly reducing the numbers of human casualties from earthquakes. While their scientists continue to develop sophisticated early-warning techniques for measuring sounds from the earth's interior and fluctuations in its water levels and magnetic field, it is the wisdom gleaned from their history books which is largely credited with saving so much human life and with making China's earthquake prediction system a model for serious study by international geophysical teams.

Generations ago Chinese farmers noticed that barnyard animals and pets seemed to go wild some hours before an earthquake. 'Normally placid horses reared and raced, dogs howled, fish leaped, and animals that were rarely seen, like snakes and rats, suddenly surged from their hiding places by the dozens' (66, p. 80).

Further research, inspired by the Chinese example, to see if such erratic animal behaviour had been noticed before earthquakes in other countries has turned up an impressive collection of data. Before the 1963 earthquake in Montana, great flocks of birds evacuated the area several hours before the first tremor. Hours before the Chilean quake of 1964, all the seagulls flew several miles out to sea. Several days before the first tremor of the 1969 Tashkent (USSR) quake, lions and tigers at the local zoo insisted on sleeping out in the open and the mountain goats refused to go into their pens. One hour before the quake, ants abandoned their anthills, carrying their pupae with them. The night before the California earthquake of 1971, rats were observed running wild in the gutters of the streets of San Fernando.

The same sort of erratic animal behaviour has been noticed preceding other natural disasters – volcanoes, hurricanes, tornados, avalanches, etc., and no one as yet fully understands the curious forecasting abilities of the species concerned. It may well be that to some extent these animals and birds are relying on some sort of psychic precognition, but here we are on the still uncharted ground of some classes of animal behaviour which J. B. Rhine, writing in the early 1950s, felt it wise to approach with caution (60).

After noting that such eminent zoologists as Sir Alister Hardy, Sir Julian Huxley and F. B. Sumner had all concluded that some sort of extrasensory perception might have to be taken into account when trying to explain such mysteries as the migratory return of salmon over thousands of miles, or the long-distance migrations and remarkable homing abilities of birds, Rhine warned that much that seems strange in animal behaviour may one day be explained quite normally when we know more about their senses. Experience has largely borne him out.

Biological research over the past twenty-five years has turned up a substantial array of straightforward scientific explanations for a great deal of previously mysterious animal behaviour.

We now know that bats navigate so well in the dark because they are sensitive to supersonic vibrations in the air; that fish can employ echo-sounding off the sea-bed; that bees and ants use polarized light in monitoring direction; and that both birds and fish can orient themselves using the angle of the sun (or the stars). Recently, scientists have made the important discovery that birds, and even man (52, pp. 844–6) are sensitive to magnetic lines of force issuing from the earth, and that by following these they can orient themselves in any direction, even if handicapped by total darkness or blindfolds.

Thus, as some writers have suggested, the disaster-predicting abilities of many animal species may be more a case of 'supersensory' than of 'extrasensory' perception. According to naturalist Ivan Sanderson, 'Such acute awareness may detect approaching hurricanes by water-level fluctuations or drops in barometric pressure. Slight sounds or a rise in temperature may herald avalanches. Volcanic eruptions and earthquakes may be preceded by greater tensions in the earth's magnetic field. Animals may respond to minor trembling and small foreshocks [22].'

Indeed, experimental parapsychologist John Randall has admitted that the many recent discoveries of hitherto unknown acute and 'super-sensitive' sensory faculties in animals have been a field day for those sceptics who would like to dismiss any apparent instance of ESP as another remnant of mere ignorance, so that many biologists 'regard the term "extra-sensory perception" as merely an admission of our ignorance, and argue that as biological knowledge expands so the number of cases of ESP will diminish.' (3, p. 79). The same argument, of course, is put forward about supposed ESP abilities in man – that one day we will understand them as part of our normal biological apparatus.

But as Randall, like Rhine and others before him, points out, there are many instances of reported ESP in animals which give good grounds for supposing that the 'undiscovered senses' thesis may prove inadequate, and these have become fruitful fields of study for experimental parapsychologists in the last decade. Most have to do with cases of apparent animal precognition, or with some kind of man–animal telepathy.*

The earliest well-documented case of supposed telepathy between a domestic animal and its trainer is the classic example from the last century of 'Clever Hans', the performing horse who, allegedly, could count, do arithmetic problems, and read letters from wooden alphabet blocks. The possibility that Clever Hans was in fact a superintelligent beast able to think through the mathematical and spelling problems set for him was discounted once it was discovered he could never get the correct answer unless there was a human being present who also knew the answer. Thus the possibility of telepathy was raised, though that too was soon dismissed with a discovery that has borne on much subsequent work on supposed telepathy between animals and humans. The secret of Clever Hans' ability, like that of Lady, a 'mind reading horse' investigated by Rhine and his wife, it turned out, was a highly developed knack for picking up subtle sensory clues from the humans around him.

Much the same sensory cue mechanism was eventually found to be

---

*Telepathy is discussed alongside precognition in the following pages on the assumption (made by many parapsychologists) that the two faculties are related and that anything we can learn about one may help us to understand the other.

opering in the case of Lady. Like Clever Hans, Lady appeared to glean telepathically the answers to various mathematical and alphabetical questions put to her by the Rhines, but in the end they discovered that she was in fact reading cues from subtle movements of their own bodies.

Although there are myriad other reported cases of animals demonstrating telepathic or clairvoyant ability, the only one still regarded as perhaps giving grounds for further consideration is that of 'Chris the Wonder Dog', who underwent stringent tests at the Duke University Parapsychological Laboratory in the 1950s and 1960s.

After noticing that Chris's early, promising problem-solving results were yet again explicable on grounds of sensory cues, the laboratory workers experimenting with him set him the task of guessing through a pack of randomly shuffled ESP cards, having him tap his paw once for a circle, twice for a square, etc. When Chris scored well above chance on this test, he was set the harder problem of guessing such cards after they had been sealed in opaque envelopes. Over one series of 500 trials, the dog scored at odds 1000 to 1 against chance, though in later trials his success rate was far less dramatic.

Rhine's colleague J. G. Pratt worked for a time with Chris, and was unable to disprove in any conclusive way that the dog was not indeed clairvoyant, but Pratt remained cautious and warned that there were other possible explanations – such, for instance, that it was the humans working with Chris who had the ESP ability, and the information thus picked up by them was then being passed on to the dog by means of sensory cues.

Summing up the many spontaneous accounts and laboratory tests on supposed telepathy of the mind-reading sort between animals and humans, experimentalist Robert Morris comments, 'Chris's case is the best of its kind. The others are somewhat impressive collectively, but individually suffer from uncertainty as to whether or not sensory cues and experimenter bias were adequately eliminated.' (84, p. 697).

There remains, however, a class of apparent man–animal telepathy for which there seems to be no alternative explanation. These are the instances of what Rhine and his daughter, Sarah Feather, dubbed 'psi-trailing', cases of where 'an animal, separated from a person or mate to which it has become attached, follows the departed companion into wholly unfamiliar territory and does so at a time and under conditions that would allow the use of no sensory trail' (61). The distances involved in the suspected instances of psi-trailing vary from 30 miles to

The Delphic Oracle. Ancient Greeks travelled for miles to hear the oracles given by young priestesses of Apollo (Pythia) who inhaled vapours to enhance their precognitive trance states.

MICHEL NOSTRADAMUS.

Médecin,

Né à St. Remy, en Provence, le 14 Décemb. 1503.
Mort le 2 juillet 1566.

Michael De Nostredame, 'Nostradamus', the sixteenth
century French physician and mystic whose name is linked
more than any other in the popular mind with prophecy and
prevision. Several of his disturbing quatrains appear to
foretell events in our own century.

The I Ching

OR

BOOK OF CHANGES

The Richard Wilhelm Translation
rendered into English by Cary F. Baynes

Foreword by C. G. Jung

Preface to the Third Edition
by Hellmut Wilhelm

London
ROUTLEDGE & KEGAN PAUL LTD

Compiled over 4000 years ago in China by Confucius and other scholars, the *I Ching* has been consulted ever since by philosophers, politicians, businessmen, and simple peasants who seek insight and guidance about their future acts. Fascinated by the book's uncanny link with unconscious forces in the mind, Jung wrote a Foreword for the celebrated Wilhelm translation.

The Welsh village of Aberfan suffered one of the worst disasters in mining history when a coaltip (seen in the background) slid down and crushed the Pantglas Junior School in 1966, killing 144 people, most of them children. Some 35 people reported having a precognitive warning of the disaster.

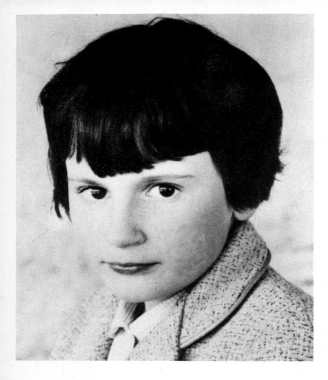

Eryl Mai Jones, the 10 year old Welsh pupil at Aberfan's Pantglas Junior School who reportedly dreamt of her school's destruction and of her own death.

On April 15, 1912, the showpiece luxury liner *Titanic* sank in the icy waters of the North Atlantic after striking an iceberg. Despite the ship's alleged invincibility, many people reported experiencing premonitory and precognitive warnings that she was headed for disaster.

The British liner *Lusitania* was sunk by a German U-Boat on May 7, 1915, with a loss of 1198 lives, but there were premonitive warnings.

Dame Edith Lyttelton, playwright and writer and a prominent member of the Cross-Correspondences circle, submitted many automatic scripts ostensibly dictated from the spirit world. One of her scripts indicated fire and trouble on the *Lusitania* a year before she was sunk.

Juliet Lady Rhys Williams, one-time Governor of the BBC and an active figure in British politics, was reported to have had several auditory premonitions, during some of which she 'heard' radio broadcasts about events that had yet to happen.

J.W. Dunne (second from left) the aeronautics engineer whose methodical recording of his own precognitive dreams in *An Experiment With Time* (1927) offered the first serious and systematic study of precognition.

Carl Gustav Jung, one of the founding fathers of twentieth century psychoanalysis, was intrigued by psychical research throughout his life. His Theory of Synchronicity (Chapter 7) attempted to explain how something like precognition was possible, and in many ways it anticipated later attempts to apply quantum theory to psychical events.

Albert Einstein's Theory of Relativity confounded all classical
and common sense notions of time, and in the wake of his
work the mere possibility of precognition no longer had to be
regarded as a conceptual heresy. But Einstein was never at
peace with some of the wider implications of the new physics,
particularly the quantum theory's prediction of
'action-at-a-distance.'

some journeys of almost 3,000 miles, and there are scores of these on record.

The case of 'Tony', a mongrel dog belonging to the Doolen family in America, is one of the best documented and most frequently cited. The Doolens originally lived in Aurora, Illinois, and when the family moved to Lansing, Michigan, over 300 miles away, they decided to leave Tony behind with a neighbour. Six weeks later the dog turned up on their Lansing doorstep, covering all those miles unaided and locating his family in a place he had never been before. Tony was still wearing his Illinois licence tag bearing his name, and the family with whom he had been left in Aurora confirmed that he was no longer with them.

Smoky, a Persian cat with a unique tuft of red hair under his chin, was parted from his family at a roadside stop in Oklahoma some 18 miles from home. The cat found his way home within a week, but his people had moved on to Tennessee. After prowling around his old neighbourhood for several weeks, Smoky disappeared, and a year later turned up at the new home of his family in Tennessee – 300 miles away.

Sugar was another Persian cat, with a distinctive callus on his hip. When his family moved from California to Oklahoma, they left Sugar with neighbours. Two weeks later he disappeared, and after fourteen months turned up on the Oklahoma doorstep of his original family, having travelled 1,500 miles. But even that remarkable distance was doubled in the best-documented case of an instance of psi-trailing in cats, a cat belonging to a New York vet. This cat was left behind when his owner got a new posting in California, but after several months he managed to track the vet down in his new home, 3,000 miles away. The cat could be identified by a distinctive bone growth on the fourth vertebra of its tail which it had sustained as the result of an earlier injury.

In their rigorous 1963 survey of psi-trailing cases (61), Rhine and Feather sifted through the scores of anecdotal reports that had been collected at Duke University over the years, and in the end decided that 25 cases met their criteria for proof of identification, believability of the general details, and supporting data from corroborating witnesses. The twenty-five consisted of ten dogs, twelve cats and three birds, all of whom had managed to trace their owners in new homes over distances of several hundred miles.

To date, there have been no rigorous attempts to study psi-trailing under controlled laboratory conditions. As early as the 1920s experimental psychologists and parapsychologists conducted field tests to measure the success rates of various animals – cats, dogs and mice – in finding their way back home from unfamiliar sites. The experiments have been repeated over half a century and the animals tested have shown a fairly consistent ability to return home from distances of between five and ten miles away, but given the deeper scientific understanding we have today of animal sensory capacities (i.e. magnetic sense, polarized light sensitivity, and sonar ability), such feats probably have very little to do with ESP.

In the 1962 Rhine and Feather survey of anecdotal accounts suggesting ESP in animals, those other than psi-trailing which were judged worthy of further consideration all involved some form of animal precognition – an early reaction to impending danger for either the animal or its owner, anticipation of a master's imminent death, or excitement at the prospect of a master's early return home.

Several examples of animals appearing to foresee imminent death have already been described, and anecdotes about the other sorts of animal precognition abound. There are, for instance, reported cases of dogs barking or refusing to leave parked cars only minutes before some natural catastrophe such as a falling tree devastated the site where they or their masters might have walked. A cat which usually slept beside the family television set, one evening jumped up, stared hard at the set and then demanded to be let out of the sitting room – several minutes later the picture tube exploded, spraying fragmented glass everywhere.

And during the Blitz, it is reported, many British relied on their cats for knowing when to seek shelter from an impending German bombing raid. Minutes before the Luftwaffe bombers could be picked up on English radar and an alarm sounded, family cats, their hair standing on end, were said to give the lead and race towards the bomb shelters. Several such life-saving cats were awarded the Dickin Medal complete with the engraving, 'We also serve' (66, pp. 82—3).

The best-researched of these many anecdotal accounts of supposed life saving by seemingly prescient pets is another war-time case discovered by Andrew MacKenzie and involves a cocker spaniel named Merry, owned by the Baines family of Wimbledon in South London.

In the early days of the war, the Baines family had sought shelter from German bombing raids in an underground shelter dug out in their back garden. But from 1941 until mid-1944, the garden shelter had been abandoned because of its dampness, in favour of a reinforced steel shelter inside the house, under the kitchen table. For nearly four years the family and a neighbour from two doors away had slept safely in the inside shelter and had seen no reason to change this habit until apparently urged to do so by Merry.

On 30 June, 1944, twelve hours after a German flying bomb had fallen on houses a block away and blown out the windows of the Baines house, Merry disappeared. After much searching, she was found curled up in the disused garden shelter. The Baines's daughter Audrey recovered the dog and refixed the pile of planks which were intended to prevent access to the garden shelter, but three more times that day Merry made her way into it and seemed reluctant to leave. At last, for reasons they later admitted were impossible to justify rationally, the Baineses decided to follow Merry's lead. They scrubbed out the garden shelter, put clean things on the bunks and that night, accompanied by their neighbour, slept within its protective walls.

At 2.50 AM the following morning, a bomb fell outside the Baines's home, destroyed and set fire to the gas mains in the road, and demolished the Baines's and several adjacent houses on the road. Had the family been sleeping in their indoor, kitchen shelter, they would all have been killed (43, pp. 81–8).

There seems no doubt from the many eye-witness reports that MacKenzie collected from the local air raid warden, members of the Baines family and some of their neighbours that the behaviour of Merry the dog did indeed save the lives of the Baines family and that of their neighbour; but was it a case of genuine precognition on Merry's part? There remains the alternative explanation that the previous night's bombing raid, which had shattered the windows in the Baines house and cracked the ceiling plaster, had been too close for Merry's comfort and, acting from good common sense and a memory of earlier security the dog had decided simply that the garden shelter was a better haven from future bombs.

With anecdotal accounts of supposed ESP in animals, as with so many involving humans, there is no definite way to answer such a question, and hence the eagerness of experimental parapsychologists to test such powers under laboratory conditions. And while so many anecdotal cases elude any sort of laboratory verification, those involving apparent precognition in animals about to be threatened with danger have in fact lent themselves to controlled experimental replication. Dr Robert Morris of the Psychical Research Foundation designed the first such tests in 1967, with moderately successful results.

Acting on the knowledge that rats exposed to danger will 'freeze', Morris created an experimental setup which could measure the rate of activity of rats in an 'open field' (unrestricted area) situation ten minutes before some of their number were about to die. One by one Morris released each of 19 test rats into the open field area and measured how many square tiles each would cover during a period of two minutes. Ten minutes later a laboratory assistant arbitrarily killed those which had been assigned an odd number by a random number generator.

When Morris checked the activity rates of all the rats against that of those selected for killing, he did indeed find a greater than chance correlation between those which 'froze' and those which died, thus apparently demonstrating a precognitive link between the rats' decreased activity and their impending death. But there are none the less grounds for caution in drawing such definite conclusions from his results. When Helmut Schmidt tried to duplicate Morris's tests in his own laboratory in Texas, he failed to get significant results of any kind; and when the Canadian researchers James Craig and William Treurinet repeated the tests, they got a greater than chance correlation between those rats which 'froze' and those which were allowed to *live* – i.e., they got a result exactly the opposite of Morris.

Again, there were apparently successful laboratory precognition experiments done in France on mice about to be subjected to mild electric shock, the aim being to find out whether the mice would act to avoid entering part of a cage where they might in future receive a shock – though which part that was to be had yet to be decided by a random number generator and the French experimenters (who preferred to write under the pseudonyms 'Duval and Montredon') obtained positive results at odds greater than 1000 to 1 against chance in their tests; but the only place their work was successfully repeated was at the Duke University laboratories by Walter Levy – and Levy's seemingly fine mouse precognition work was later exposed as rank fraud by J. B. Rhine and others. In fact the Levy fraud is one of the worst cases of cheating to occur in experimental psychology.

Thus, while there has been some small promise in laboratory studies of animal precognition, there is as yet no one piece of research which has been so solid, and so consistently repeatable, as to provide any really impressive experimental proof that the phenomenon does indeed exist. There remain anecdotes from daily life which suggest that some animals do, at some times, display what appears to be ESP ability of one sort or another; but if this is indeed the case there is still no proof to suggest that they do so any more frequently or more reliably than humans. In 1974 John Beloff, a psychologist at the University of Edinburgh and a former President of the SPR summed up the current state of experimental knowledge by saying, somewhat disparagingly (3, p. 77), 'Such evidence as we have on animal psi (ESP), and it is very exiguous even as compared with that on human psi, suggests that psi is just as exceptional in its occurrence and just as marginal in its effects in the former as in the latter.'

6 The Psychology of Precognition

While some parapsychologists have been busying themselves with trying to establish whether a phenomenon such as precognition does in fact exist at all, others have concentrated more of their attention on the psychology of the subject: *who* has precognition? and under what emotional or mental circumstances?

Both the giants of modern psychology, Freud and Jung, were at some point involved in parapsychological research, and published many papers on the subject. But while such an interest came naturally, almost passionately to Jung early in his career (his inaugural dissertation for his medical degree was a study of 'The Psychology and Pathology of So-Called Occult Phenomena'), Freud came to the field almost despite himself, like an unwilling conscript who had failed every means of draft evasion.

In his autobiography, *Memories, Dreams and Reflections*, Jung relates the story of an incident which happened when he travelled to Vienna in 1909 to seek Freud's views on precognition and other parapsychological interests. At the mention of the subject, Freud fell into a tirade against the 'black tide of mud, of occultism' and would hear no word of good about such matters. As Jung told the story,

> While Freud was going on in this way, I had a curious sensation. It was as if my diaphragm were made of iron and were becoming red hot – a glowing vault. And at that moment there was such a loud report in the bookcase, which stood right next to us, that we both started up in alarm, fearing the thing was going to topple over on us. I said to Freud:
> 'There, that is an example of a so-called catalytic exteriorization phenomenon.'
> 'Oh come,' he exclaimed. 'That is sheer bosh.'
> 'It is not,' I replied. 'You are mistaken, Herr Professor. And to prove my point I now predict that in a moment there will be another loud report!' Sure enough, no sooner had I said the words than the same detonation went off in the bookcase.
> To this day I do not know what gave me this certainty. But I knew

beyond all doubt that the report would come again. Freud only stared aghast at me. I do not know what was in his mind or what his look meant. In any case, this incident aroused his mistrust of me, and I had the feeling that I had done something against him. I never afterwards discussed the incident with him. [35, p. 152]

But while Jung's impulse was to shy away from any further discussion of psychic phenomena with Freud after the bookcase incident, Freud himself did refer to the matter again, quite soon after, in an avuncular letter to Jung. After jovially explaining away the noises which had emanated from his bookcase during their meeting, he admonished his young protégé about his interests in 'occultism' and advised him, 'to keep a cool head and rather not understand something than make such great sacrifices for the sake of understanding' (35, Appendix).

It was not clear whether Freud felt Jung would be sacrificing his reputation or his sanity (or both) in pursuing the occult; but Freud's own clinical experiences worked against his dogged resistance to parapsychology. Telepathic occurrences between himself and his patients were too numerous, and try as he would, he could not explain them away. He became more open-minded to the research being done in the field, and when he learned of experiments carried out with Professor Gilbert Murray, whom he knew to be a distinguished Oxford don, he capitulated. In an enthusiastic letter to Ernest Jones he declared, 'I confess that the immediate impression made by these reports was so strong that . . . I should be prepared to lend the support of psychoanalysis to the matter of telepathy.' The more conservative Jones was mortified by such a suggestion, feeling certain it would destroy the reputation of psychoanalysis; but there was no restraining the master now. In 1911 he became a member of both the British and American Societies for Psychical Research, and he published his first (of many) paper on telepathy in 1922.

Freud's major preoccupation was with the psychodynamic conditions which best gave rise to psychic experiences, and to finding some place for them within his general personality theory. In the end, he concluded that they were archaic and regressive capacities held over from a much earlier period in human development:

Telepathy may be the original archaic means through which individuals understood one another; a means pushed into the background, in the course of phylogenetic development, by a better method of communication, that is to say by signs perceived by the sensory organs. But these older methods of communication may have survived in the background and may still manifest themselves under certain conditions. [21]

In his own study of precognition, H. F. Saltmarsh suggested what these certain conditions might be. 'In my opinion,' he wrote, 'precognitions occur only when the subject is in a state of dissociation, that is to say, they are affairs of the subliminal, or the subconscious mind' (64, p. 14). Certainly there is plenty of evidence for this view.

The shaman prophets of the Neolithic era stocked the fires of their previsionary images by meditating on the whirling birds of the swastika symbol which, when rotated in a clockwise direction, was believed to release the forces of the unconscious. The whirling dervishes of Islam, the priestesses of Delphi and all the early Biblical prophets worked themselves up into states of ecstasy or dementia through music or drugged vapours in order to enhance their prophetic gifts through greater contact with their own non-rational selves; and in his *Timaeus*, Plato reflected that all this was the intended design of Nature. The authors of our being, he concluded, had seated the prophetic gift in the liver because this organ was in the lower part of the body and divination was a power rightly attributed to the lower orders of our nature:

> No man, when in his wits, attains prophetic truth and inspiration, but when he receives the inspired word, either his intelligence is enthralled in sleep or he is demented by some distemper or possession . . . For this reason it is customary to appoint interpreters to be judges of the true inspirations (who are) the expositors of dark sayings and visions.
>
> *Timaeus*, 71$_c$–72$_b$

This general view that the powers of ESP are in some way primitive, subconscious or archaic throwbacks is mirrored in the work of many psychiatrists who, referring to the voices and visions of the mentally ill, particularly schizophrenics, argue that such faculties are signs of some mental aberration. 'Unless one has had personal contact with people claiming psychic experiences,' Professor D. J. West has observed in his comprehensive survey of spontaneous cases of precognition (81, pp. 264–300), 'it may be difficult to imagine what insanity has to do with the subject.' But 'it is by no means unknown for SPR officials to have to deal with wild-eyed callers who claim to be in constant telepathic rapport with something or somebody . . . There are actually thousands of patients in (and out of) asylums, the main features of whose illness is an obsession by imaginary psychic entities.' But West would agree that insanity *per se*, where people are suffering delusions of psychic experience rather than being open to genuine psychic experiences, is the less interesting side of the question of how ESP ability might relate to mental instability. The thesis that such a genuine ability may itself be symptomatic of a breakdown in some normal screening faculties possessed by the majority of minds is more to the point.

This notion of 'screening faculties' comes from the work of the philosopher Henri Bergson, who suggested that our nervous system is designed as an elaborate filter, intended to let through those energies and 'radiations' which are of use to us in developing our higher intellectual faculties, and coping with what we experience. Bergson's 'filter' is like Kant's categories of perception and understanding; both philosophers suggest that the reality beyond these categories, or filters, contains all sorts of things inaccessible to us, structured as we are.

The 'primitive faculties' view of ESP suggested by Freud – and supported by the clinical work of psychoanalyst Jan Ehrenwald, who demonstrated a high correlation between psychic ability and the early signs of nascent schizophrenia and other forms of psychosis – assumes that faculties such as telepathy and precognition had to be sacrificed for the sake of human evolution. The awareness of reality generated by such throwback faculties 'is dim and uncertain', Ehrenwald explained, 'subject to errors of refraction, as it were, caused by the vagaries of the unconscious strata of the mind through which they have to pass.' In order that our more precise logical and linguistic faculties should develop (and perhaps even for our survival as a species to be assured), such hit-and-miss quasi-perception had to be blocked out from our everyday conscious awareness. As Sir Cyril Burt, Professor of Psychology at University College, London, described the position in a 1968 address to the British Society for Psychical Research:

> ''Osses,' said the coachman to Tom Brown, ''as to wear blinkers, so's they see only wot's in front of 'em: and that's the safest plan for 'umble folk like you and me.' Nature seems to have worked on much the same principle. Our sense organs and our brain operate as an intricate kind of filter which limits and directs the mind's clairvoyant powers, so that under normal conditions attention is concentrated on just those objects or situations that are of biological importance for the survival of the organism and its species . . . As a rule, it would seem, the mind rejects ideas coming from another mind as the body rejects grafts coming from another body. [38, p. 132]

Yet while stating the probable necessity for such a blinkered approach to reality, Burt was quick to point out that, 'to suppose that on such a basis we can construct a complete and all-inclusive picture of the universe is like supposing that a street-plan of Rome will tell you what the Eternal City looks like when you get there.'

The view that extra-sensory faculties like telepathy and precognition are a primitive throwback is, however, by no means a unanimous one. Other psychologists strongly disagree and argue that ESP is either some natural, though neglected, part of our normal psychic make-up; or that it is indeed some new 'sixth sense', towards the increasing mastery of which we are evolving. Writing at the end of the last century, one of the founders of the SPR, Frederic Myers, thought that this new faculty would expand our awareness far beyond the boundaries of normal human experience as we know it today; and half a century later the controversial philosopher C. E. M. Joad argued that it was 'a first faltering intimation of a new thrust forward on the part of a purposive life force.'

Research into the Psychology of ESP

Whether ESP is in fact some regressive faculty harking back to the dark ages of our primitive past, outmoded, embarrassing and a sure sign of mental instability, or whether it is symptomatic of some bright new tomorrow, is a debate which has shaped much of the psychologically-oriented research in experimental parapsychology over the past twenty-five years. Researchers have hoped that if they could accumulate enough data about the types of people (their age, mental state, degree of civilization, etc.) most likely to experience ESP and the psychological and physiological conditions most conducive to their experiencing it, the question might be settled once and for all.

Freud's thesis that ESP is an atavistic phenomenon more appropriate to the life-styles of savages than to highly evolved, civilized man has suggested three obvious targets for experimental research: animals; those few 'savage peoples' still scattered about in distant parts of Africa and Southeast Asia; and our own children before they reach intellectual maturity.

If ESP is a for the most part vanishing capacity belonging further down the phylogenetic scale then, some psychologists have reasoned, we ought surely to find it being more prevalent in the lower animals; and indeed tales about the alleged psychic capacities of both wild and domestic animals are abundant. But for all their trying, experimentalists have in fact been able to produce very little hard evidence that animals experience telepathy or precognition. Thus evidence for Freud's thesis would have to lie elsewhere, and anthropology has looked a promising field to try.

Anthropological Research

Just as the myths and legends from earlier stages of our own culture were dominated by tales of witches and seers invested with extraordinary powers for reading people's thoughts, foresight, levitation, etc., so much of anthropological lore in the early part of this century was strongly inspired by reports of 'psychic savages' appearing in the travel commentaries of explorers. As anthropologists made more field trips to such places as Borneo, Haiti, Cape Town and the Congo, they came back armed with anecdotes about mediumistic seances, Voodoo ecstasy rites during which levitation regularly occurred, and miraculous reports of crucial information travelling hundreds of miles through the bush almost instantaneously.

A diviner in South Africa was said to have predicted correctly to one anthropologist that a pregnant black goat about which he was concerned would soon give birth to a grey and white kid; the Tembu (Cape Town) diviner Solomon Baba was said to have guessed correctly that, before coming to visit him from sixty miles away, the South African psychiatrist Laubscher had buried a small purse wrapped in brown paper under a flat brown stone which in turn had been covered by a grey stone (84, pp. 672–3); half an hour before the Jamaican earthquake of 1907, a mulatto girl was said to have broken into convulsive sobs and run through the streets shouting, 'Something dreadful is going to happen'; and during the devastating 1951 hurricane in Jamaica, people deprived of all normal means of distant communication were said to have contacted each other across the island in some 'natural and mysterious' way, while one mother was said successfully to have sent a message to her endangered children ten miles away by relaying it through the good offices of a cotton tree (85, pp. 103, 105).

Yet in all these accounts, the common denominator is that the evidence is anecdotal, and those by whom such things were said were the natives, who were found invariably to believe in the veracity of their own and their kinsfolks' psychic capacities. Many early anthropologists unashamedly contended that such testimony was good enough for them. As Robert Lowie put it,

The accounts of occult experiences by otherwise intelligent and trustworthy reporters cannot simply be brushed aside. They ring true, whatever may be the interpretations of visions and auditions. As my best Crow interpreter phrased it, 'When you listen to the old men telling about their mysterious experiences, you've just *got* to believe them. [84, p. 671]

And Lowie's high regard for any belief so widely shared was supported by Ralph Linton, (84, p. 671), who wrote,

I have been struck, myself, in my experience with primitive groups, with the surprising uniformity of their stories about what we would call psychic phenomena. Beliefs regarding these phenomena coming from groups which could have had no possible contact are, nevertheless, so much alike that they suggest either an amazing limitation on the human imagination, or the presence of a common basis of observed fact.

Students of modern psychical research might recognize this 'if so many people believe it, it must be true,' line of argument, but they will also know that the more critical activists in the field have demanded some more objective standards of proof. And so it has been amongst anthropologists in the past three decades.

A Dutch psychologist, Dr M. Pobers, used the format of an international symposium on extrasensory perception (85) to criticize (in perhaps purposively tendentious terms) the often naïve credulity of anthropologists and psychologists who have studied the rituals and beliefs of primitive peoples, and called for the application of more objective – and if possible, more experimental – study techniques. He was not the first to point out that researchers who go along to native meetings in the jungle, where their senses are subjected to the incessant, rhythmic beating of drums and the inhalation of heavy and intoxicating fumes are likely to become emotionally involved in the proceedings. At one such meeting which he attended in Haiti, a woman possessed by the spirit of the occasion jumped six feet into the air and then suspended herself from a beam for several minutes.

'The same phenomenon observed from a slightly different angle,' commented Pobers, 'could have been described as levitation,' and he implies it was clearly intended to be seen as such. But does that mean that Haitian witch doctors (for example) might be keeping alive the myth of the psychic savage at least in part through those kinds of simulation and fraud which have at times disgraced the performances of 'public psychics' in our own culture? Judging by the testimony of one such witch doctor, it would seem so.

'In the west,' the Haitian told Pobers, 'money leads to power: here power leads to money. A diviner cannot afford in his practice "hits and misses". Even if his powers are genuine, he must be a master of simulation and fraud. This is his unemployment insurance [78, p. 109].'

To get round the problem of being fooled by such intended simulation or by the more innocent but equally misleading blind faith which members of primitive groups tend to have in their own psychic powers, Pobers called for on-the-spot laboratory style testing for the actual level of psychic capability amongst primitive peoples. A few such studies have been done.

In 1949, Ronald and Lyndon Rose travelled to the Woodenbong Aboriginal Settlement in New South Wales, Australia to carry out a series of standard ESP card-guessing experiments with the natives. They had been told by the Aborigines that in crisis situations, such as the death or serious illness of a close relative, telepathic communication was a reliable and commonplace experience. But in their Rhine-style tests (296 in all) in which twenty-three Aborigines of all ages were asked to guess which of five possible types of cards was being selected from the pack of twenty-five, the results were inconclusive. One Aborigine subject, an old lady of seventy-seven, scored very highly above chance, but eighteen showed no deviation from chance expectation and the other four only marginal deviation (63). The Roses also asked the same group of subjects to attempt a psychokinesis experiment in which they were to use their minds to attempt to influence the way in which a series of dice would fall when shaken, but this experiment produced no results outside chance expectation. The Aborigines told the Roses they shouldn't have expected otherwise on the dice experiment, because 'only clever men can do things like that.'

The Roses tried ESP card-guessing tests on native tribesmen in Samoa, but got no results above chance expectation; nor did another anthropologist, Jeffrey Mason, who tried the tests on Liberian tribesmen, get significant results.

In 1968 and 1974, Robert L. Van de Castle tested a total of 461 adolescent Cuna Indian students from the San Blas Islands off the coast of Panama for ESP ability using a set of specially designed cards bearing such symbols as sharks, jaguars and canoes because these objects meant more to his subjects than those on the standard Zener cards. The 96 girls whom he tested scored very marginally above chance expectation, and the 365 boys very marginally below. In the case of both sexes, youngsters tested more than once tended to score even more closely to chance, though in looking at his series of tests as a whole, Van de Castle felt his results significant enough to merit further investigation (84, pp. 678–80).

Thus the western-style ESP tests, when practised on subjects drawn from various primitive groups, while potentially meaningful, were certainly not sufficiently spectacular to justify any claims that 'savages' are more psychic than civilized man. But few conclusions can be drawn from such test results. Bearing in mind that the Aborigines tested by the Roses, for instance, had claimed that their telepathic abilities were best demonstrated in crisis situations, it may well be that they simply found the card-guessing experiments far too boring, or too alien to their way of doing things, to perform well on them. The 'boredom factor' has certainly played a significant part in dampening the performances of western subjects subjected to the dull and repetitive runs of card-guessing experiments.

Research with Children
In Britain, Ernesto Spinelli, who did extensive research for his PhD thesis at the University of Surrey (69) into the question of whether young children (in our own culture) are more telepathic than their elders, tried to get around the problem of boredom or alienation having a negative effect on possible ESP results by conducting his experiments in a party atmosphere. He allowed his subjects to wear a dramatic-looking 'thinking cap' while they vied with each other to win 'The Guessing Game' and reap a reward of fistfuls of Smarties. Nearly fifty years earlier, Louisa Rhine had thought along similar lines (with very successful results) by inventing an ESP game for young children.

The notion that young children might be more open to extrasensory perception would be a likely upshot of Freud's thesis that ESP is an atavistic phenomenon, and the truth of it has appeared to be borne out by clinical work with children since. C. D. Broad thought that some form of telepathy, at least, was partly responsible for the special intuitive skills demonstrated by youngsters during those early years when they have so much to learn from both their parents and teachers. And Jan Ehrenwald, who agreed that some such faculty is part of normal communication between young children and their mothers at least, felt that his work with disturbed youngsters provided even stronger evidence for an openness to extrasensory phenomena. He noted that, again and again, children aged three and four seemed to have a working knowledge of thoughts and symbols (particularly sexual) more appropriate to adults, and that the things which filled these children's heads was often closely related to whatever lay at the root of their disturbed mothers' problems.

Rita, aged three, was suffering from an obsessional neurosis which seemed to duplicate most of the symptoms of a similar neurosis found in her mother, including its hidden (adult-type) sexual implications . . . Peter, aged three, was likewise suffering from a neurosis with all the paraphernalia of sexual symbolism of adult type . . . The mother of a feeble-minded sixteen-year-old girl (underwent) psychological treatment, and while the analysis of the mother made satisfactory progress the mental condition of her daughter, too, seemed to improve. [17, pp. 192–3]

'However,' Ehrenwald noted, 'in the course of gradual development and consolidation of the personality of the growing child this susceptibility to telepathy and related influences recedes more and more into the background.' It was to test this kind of clinical impression that Spinelli set out to put his child subjects through their experimental paces.

Spinelli drew his subjects, aged three onwards, from local nursery and primary schools and tested them in pairs. Each child was given a box encasing five buttons he might push, one for each of five possible pictures displayed on a card. When one child chose a picture and indicated his choice by pushing a button, the other child (seated opposite and unable to see what his partner was doing) was asked to guess which picture his partner had chosen and to register his guess by pushing the relevant button on his own box. Each time a correct guess was registered, a bell rang to congratulate the child and encourage him.

Each session (Spinelli did 1,200 in all over the course of five years) consisted of the children taking turns to guess which of five symbols the other had chosen on a run of twenty cards. The cards themselves were arranged in order by reference to random number tables, and each guess was registered electronically on a chart recorder to eliminate cheating or experimenter error. The results were dramatic, and would seem to contribute hard experimental evidence for Freud's thesis that ESP ability belongs to an earlier stage of human development.

By dividing his child subjects into four age groupings – 3–3½ years, 4½–5 years, 5–7 years, and 8 years onwards – and testing for telepathic communication between the children themselves in each group as measured by successful guessing of the picture cards, Spinelli was able to establish that as children get older and their brains' conceptual abilities mature, their ability to communicate telepathically apparently declines.

Thus in the youngest group tested, the 3–3½-year-olds, the children guessed correctly 27% above chance expectation. In the 4½–5-year-olds this fell to 15%, in the 5–7-year-olds to 4%, and from 8 years onwards the children's correct guessing was just what would be expected by chance. These results, which are similar to an earlier study done on older Dutch schoolchildren and which have to some extent been duplicated by Dr Michael Winkleman at the University of California, may help to shed further light on both human mental development and the nature of ESP ability.

EEG (electroencephalogram) research over the past two decades has clearly demonstrated the existence of four separate electrical wave patterns associated with the human brain: alpha, beta, theta and delta waves. Each is commonly associated with different brain functions. In most normal adult brains, the beta waves, which are associated with organized, conceptual thinking, dominate the EEG pattern during waking hours. Delta waves are found when the brain is in a state of deep, dreamless sleep; theta, during dreaming sleep; and alpha, in a state of deep relaxation, when the brain is fully awake but not focusing on any particular idea.

From late foetal stages until about the age of three, the human infant's brain shows an EEG pattern dominated by the very slow delta waves. From the ages of three to five, a young child's brain emits mainly theta waves, with increasing proportions of alpha waves appearing with maturity. Between the ages of five and eight, this balance between theta and alpha waves is shifting towards a dominance of alpha waves, and at the latter end of the scale the beta waves so characteristic of adult thinking begin to appear.

Thus, between the ages of three and eight, when the children in Spinelli's research groups were showing a marked ESP ability, their brain waves were apparently dominated by a mixture of theta and alpha rhythms. Perhaps significantly, these same slower brain rhythms dominate the EEG patterns of adult brain states commonly associated with ESP ability – dreaming sleep (theta waves), trance states, and meditative states, such as those reached in TM (transcendental meditation). Nearly all the cases of spontaneous precognition cited earlier took place when the person concerned was dreaming or else in some abnormal trance state, and so it may well be that the presence of alpha and theta waves is in some way a key to the nature of ESP ability.

Research Using Adults

At the Cambridge University Psychological Laboratory, Dr Carl Sargent has been investigating whether ESP ability is enhanced in adults by blocking out the kind of thinking normally associated with beta waves – concentrated, conceptual thinking. In essence, Sargent's work is similar to earlier research carried out by Charles Honorton at New York's Maimonides Hospital Dream Laboratory on ESP and hypnosis, where a high correlation between hypnotic states and ESP performance was successfully demonstrated, but Sargent subjects his adult subjects to Ganzfeld Technique (see p. 65). Like Spinelli, Sargent works with his subjects in pairs. While one is reclining in the Ganzfeld sensory deprivation chamber, another is sitting in a different room of the laboratory staring at some randomly selected visual image on a card. The experiment consists of asking the relaxed partner to describe his imagery and then to see whether this resembles in any way the symbol or picture being looked at by the active partner. So far, in 302 sessions using 100 different subjects, Sargent has found a correlation between the descriptions and the cards 14.53% above chance expectation.

Sargent describes the Ganzfeld sensory deprivation technique as increasing 'primary process thinking' – the random, spontaneous imagery most frequent in childhood. EEG studies of the Ganzfeld state are so far rudimentary, but it would seem that it does cause the brain to transmit increased numbers of alpha waves, and Sargent thinks it not unlikely that later EEG studies will show the presence of theta waves.

Relating Sargent's sensory deprivation results to his own findings with children, Spinelli says, 'I've undergone the Ganzfeld Technique myself. It blocks out all the normal ways that adults structure experience with thoughts and induces a kind of dreamy awareness. I think that's the way young children feel most of the time.'

Finally, in what could be seen as a natural extension of both Spinelli's work with children and Sargent's with sensory deprivation, a few experimental parapsychologists have been testing to determine which, if any, specific personality traits are most compatible with ESP ability. In his own laboratory at Cambridge, Sargent noticed that some of his subjects consistently did well in demonstrating telepathy during his sensory deprivation experiments, while others did consistently badly, and he wondered why this was – whether it is in fact the case that certain types of people, because of their personalities, might simply be more or less able to experience things like telepathy and precognition.

Judging from his clinical work with psychiatric patients, Jan Ehrenwald had formed the very definite view that people with a tendency to psychosis (schizophrenia) were more open to extrasensory data than people with a strong sense of their own personal identities ('high ego strength'). But in more recent years, psychologists have wondered whether there might be any repeatable experimental proof of Ehrenwald's observation, and whether the same might apply to neurosis. In other words, might a very anxious person or an obsessive person be more or less open to ESP, does it matter whether someone is outgoing (extrovert) or shy (introvert), believes in ESP or thinks the whole field is utter nonsense?

To find the answers to such questions, researchers like Gertrude Schmeidler and John Palmer in America, K. R. Rao in India and Sargent in Britain have all tried looking for definite experimental links between these and other personality traits and a person's ability to perform in some consistent manner on ESP tests. In each case, they have used Cattell's by now standard test for measuring personality traits or, in the case of Sargent, some slight variation on the Cattell test.

Cattell's test, which is used in most schools and psychological testing centres to measure both IQ and personality type, asks people a series of questions designed to draw out whether they are anxious or relaxed, outgoing or shy, trusting or suspicious, etc. Sargent's variation added a few questions to determine whether his subjects tended to believe or disbelieve in ESP, and whether they were any good at recalling their dreams or picturing things in their heads (see questionnaire, p. 103).

Altogether, the data collected by the various researchers has strongly suggested that someone who can generally recall his dreams and picture things in his head, and who is relaxed, outgoing, trusting and generally tends to believe in ESP is more likely to experience it than someone who doesn't often recall his dreams or form pictures in his head, and who is anxious, shy and suspicious. The problem with these findings, however, is that people are naturally rather complicated and few, if any, conveniently combine in their personalities all of the ESP-positive or ESP-negative traits on which the researchers have agreed.

Thus, while an ideal person whose personality was a composite of all the 'right' and 'wrong' traits might be trusted to score consistently well or badly on an ESP test, in reality such testing for purposes of finding ideal ESP subjects has been fairly inconclusive. Still, the isolation of certain personality traits which seem to be compatible with ESP ability is bound to aid the eventual understanding of just what that ability is, and the use of such personality tests for finding good ESP subjects, while not foolproof, does seem to eliminate some of the headache of unpredictability in experimental parapsychology.

QUESTIONNAIRE. Please answer ALL the questions; this is very important. Thanks.

                                                   A B C

1. I recall my dreams:
(a) less than once a week; (b) once or twice a week; (c) more often than twice a week.   0 1 2

2. For a holiday I would rather go to:
(a) a busy holiday town; (b) something in between (a) and (c); (c) a quiet cottage off the beaten track.   2 1 0

3. If I close my eyes and try to summon up a visual image of someone, I:
(a) cannot do this; (b) can do it with difficulty; (c) can do it easily   0 1 2

4. I am not much given to cracking jokes and telling funny stories:
(a) true; (b) in between; (c) false.   0 1 2

5. I tend to be critical of other people's work:
(a) yes; (b) occasionally; (c) no.   0 1 2

6. Changes in weather don't usually affect my efficiency and mood:
(a) true; (b) in between; (c) false.   2 1 0

7. I accept the possibility that extra-sensory perception might occur:
(a) yes; (b) not sure; (c) no.   2 1 0

8. I often feel quite tired when I get up in the morning:
(a) yes; (b) in between; (c) no.   0 1 2

9. If I know that someone's line of reasoning is in error, I tend to:
(a) keep quiet; (b) in between; (c) speak out.   0 1 2

10. I accept the possibility that I might be able to use extra-sensory perception in some way:
(a) yes; (b) unsure; (c) no.   2 1 0

11. When I am going to catch a train, I get a little hurried, tense, or anxious, though I know I have time:
(a) yes; (b) sometimes; (c) no.   0 1 2

12. I generally recall only fragments of dreams rather than a complete dream:
(a) yes; (b) in between; (c) no.   0 1 2

13. If I tried to conjure up an auditory image of a piece of music, I would find this:
(a) easy; (b) in between; (c) difficult or impossible.   2 1 0

14. I enjoy getting into conversation and find it easy to start talking with a stranger:
(a) true; (b) in between; (c) false.   2 1 0

Sargent's slight variation on selected questions from Cattell's personality test. Questions 5, 6, 8, and 11 tested for anxiety; 2, 4, 9, and 14, for extroversion; 3, 12, and 13, for visual imagery; and 7 and 10, for belief in ESP. If the subject scored O on a question, it meant that answer suggested negative ESP ability, whereas if he scored 2, his answer promised positive ESP ability.

Sargent then asked people taking this test to sit an ESP test, and he found that those scoring most highly in answer to the personality questions also did best on the ESP test.

7 Jung's Theory of Synchronicity

While most psychologists and psychiatrists in the first half of this century were content with collecting evidence for ESP and unravelling its psychodynamics, in the hope of fitting any observed phenomena into the right psychic pigeonhole, Jung set himself a far more difficult task. Already convinced in the early days of his medical career that such things as telepathy, precognition and psychokinesis do in fact exist, he wanted to understand *how* they could do so. The result of this effort, published towards the end of his life, was his 'Theory of Synchronicity'.

By 'synchronicity', Jung means what most people would call 'coincidence' – the tendency for things of a similar sort to pop up unexpectedly at the same time, or for things to happen in groups. But at the outset he makes a crucial distinction between 'mere chance coincidences', arbitrary groupings of superficially similar things, and 'meaningful coincidences', groups of things or events which are not arbitrary but rather which share some common meaning.

As an example of chance coincidence, he cites someone's taking a bus to the theatre and finding that not only does the theatre ticket bear the same number as the bus ticket but that both have the same series of digits that make up the telephone number of a man whom he meets for the first time in the theatre lobby that night.

'(Such) chance groupings or series seem,' Jung says, 'at least to our present way of thinking, to be meaningless, and to fall as a general rule within the limits of probability. There are, however,' he continues, 'incidents whose "chancefulness" seems open to doubt.' These latter are the incidents which illustrate what he calls meaningful coincidences, and there are probably few people to whom such things have not occurred from time to time.

We think of someone we've not seen or thought of for years, and then suddenly that person turns up; a theoretical physicist is writing a paper on the unity between the observer and what he observes in quantum physics when, while he is browsing through the public library with his wife, she arbitrarily selects a volume by an Indian guru of whom neither has heard and the books falls open at a page which argues, 'there is no distinction between the observer and the observed'; a writer submits a manuscript to a publisher through her agent and then goes off to a conference in another city where she finds that both she and the publisher have been invited for cocktails by a third person who knew nothing of the manuscript and whom neither person could have guessed knew the other. All coincidences, but of the sort Jung would call 'meaningful'.

Among doctors, Jung claims the 'duplication of cases' is another familiar phenomenon which he thinks illustrates his theory. He cites the example of a young doctor who diagnosed an instance of an extremely rare tropical disease in a patient, the kind of disease that most doctors encounter only in their medical textbooks or, at most, once in a lifetime's career. Excited by his discovery, the young doctor reported it to his professor, who commented, 'Um – the way these things happen, I wouldn't be surprised if another case turns up soon.' And sure enough, within a fortnight, the junior doctor encountered a second case of the same rare disease. The two patients had no relationship to each other, and there was no chance that either could have been contaminated by the other.

In a different sort of example, this time in connection with the strange way lost objects seem to 'find their way back' to their owners, Jung writes about the very remarkable case of a German mother who had taken a photograph of her son in the Black Forest in 1914, just before the outbreak of the First World War. She took the film to a photographer's shop to be developed, but the outbreak of war made it impossible to collect it, and eventually she accepted that she would never see the film again.

In 1916, the same woman visited another photographer's shop, this time in Frankfurt, to purchase some new film with which to photograph her baby daughter. When she took this second roll of film in to be developed, it came back to her double exposed – the pictures on top were the ones recently taken of her daughter, but the ones beneath those she had taken of her son in 1914. Her old film had somehow got back into circulation, packaged as new film, and had 'coincidentally' been purchased by its same owner twice.

And finally, in an example of the kind of coincidence which might be described as precognition, Jung relates the story of a young woman patient of his who dreamt the night before coming to see him that she had been given a golden scarab. As he sat in his study with his back to the closed window listening to this young woman describe her dream, Jung heard a gentle tapping behind his shoulder. When he looked round, he saw a small insect knocking against the window pane, and when he opened the window the insect flew in. He caught it in his hand and discovered that it was a scarabaeid beetle, or common rose chafer – the closest equivalent one could find to a golden scarab in Switzerland.

'I must admit,' he wrote, 'that nothing like it ever happened to me before or since, and that the dream of the patient has remained unique in my experience', but he 'kept coming across connections which I simply could not explain as chance groupings or "runs".'

Thus it was from his own vast clinical experience (and spurred on by the impressive telepathy and precognition results which J. B. Rhine had got in his ESP card-guessing experiments) that Jung found his main impetus to evolve some explanation for a set of phenomena for which there was not only no known, but apparently no conceivable explanation. The laws of nature, he knew, purported to rest firmly on the law of causality (according to which every effect must have a cause, and that cause must precede the effect), yet how, he asked, in a world supposedly governed by the law of causality, could there be phenomena which so clearly violated that law? His answer was to doubt, not the veracity of the phenomena, but the universal validity of the law:

'Early on, certain doubts had arisen in me as to the unlimited applicability of the causal principle in psychology . . . Causality is only one principle and psychology essentially cannot be exhausted by causal methods only.' If the law of causality couldn't accommodate the existence of certain facts associated with the workings of the mind, among them telepathy and precognition, then, Jung argued, that law must rest on a distorted or, at best, partial view of reality and was itself in need of some rethinking.

Jung was encouraged in his intuitive rebellion against causality by what he had gleaned of the new developments in twentieth-century physics. He knew that Einstein's relativity theory had challenged and upset all the old notions of space and time which were part of the causal framework, and the exceedingly curious, apparently anarchic, sub-atomic events described by quantum physics seemed to him even more directly relevant to understanding the mechanics of the psyche. He felt that if the universe were ever to be understood fully, this task would be achieved by both physics and psychology transcending the shackles of their own disciplinary limitations and moving forward together with shared insights.

> After collecting psychological experiences from many people and many countries for fifty years, I doubt whether an exclusively psychological approach can do justice to the phenomena in question. Not only the findings of parapsychology, but my own theoretical reflections . . . have led me to certain postulates which touch on the realms of nuclear physics and the conception of the space-time continuum. This opens up the whole question of the transpsychic reality immediately underlying the psyche. [33, p. 18]

Hoping to develop a more rigorous exposition of his own psychological intuitions, then, Jung took as his tutor in modern physics the Nobel prizewinning quantum physicist Wolfgang Pauli. Jung saw parapsychology as a natural bridge between physics and psychology; and Pauli, who shared this view, hoped that in working with Jung he might find a way to express on the larger scale, everyday level of reality some natural extension of the very small scale, quantum mechanical phenomena he had helped to discover.

In 1952, Jung and Pauli published their collaborative effort in *The Interpretation of Nature and the Psyche*. The book consisted of an essay by Jung entitled, 'Synchronicity: An Acausal Connecting Principle' and one by Pauli entitled, 'The Influence of Archetypal Ideas on the Scientific Theories of Kepler.' Both essays put forward the view that there is an absolute spaceless, timeless cosmos in which both the soul (or psyche) and the material universe are manifest. Pauli argued that this cosmos had an order of its own, independent of human will, human perceptual categories or our supposed laws of causality. In it, all accepted boundaries between the knower and the known broke down and mind and matter came to be seen as extensions of each other.

Jung called this somewhat mystical absolute 'transpsychic reality'; and he, too, argued that there, in a realm beyond our conscious psyche with its divisions between mind and matter and its causal perceptions manifested in space and time, there is a timeless unity in which past, present, and future merge, and where matter and the psyche are but alternative manifestations of a single reality. His theory of synchronicity stemmed from what he saw as an 'unexpected parallelism between psychic and physical events,' a kind of parallelism mirrored at the quantum level by the tendency of fundamental particles (electrons, protons, etc.) to behave sometimes like waves and sometimes like particles.

As has already been said, Jung's theory is based on the existence of meaningful coincidences, and for him, 'meaning' was the key word, providing the dynamics of synchronistic phenomena. He felt very strongly that thoughts or events which shared some common meaning (my thought of some long absent friend and that friend's unknown physical proximity, the physicist's burning interest in the question of the knower and the known and a book which takes that problem as one of its central themes) were attracted to each other almost like magnets, though there might be no orthodox causal relationship between them. Such shared meanings, Jung believed, could occasionally get joined up at the level of everyday conscious reality (as coincidences, telepathy or precognition) because 'lower down', at the level of transpsychic reality where all minds are 'plugged into' the same source, all shared meanings are synchronistically linked. The whole theory of synchronicity is bound up intrinsically with Jung's theory of the collective unconscious and the archetypes.

The basic notion running through all Jung's work is that, as a species, all humans share some common memories and experiences, and that these jointly owned racial treasures are stored away in the collective unconscious. But the memories and experiences which fill the collective unconscious are of a very special sort – they exist as archetypes, or formal patterns of psychic energy that structure the shared sense of meaning for mankind as a whole. Jung's archetypes are, at the psychological level, roughly equivalent to Plato's Forms at the conceptual level and, like Plato on the subject of thought, Jung argues that all of our unconscious life (our dreams, our impulses, our mythologies our artistic creativity, etc.) mirrors the world of pure archetypes, drawing its psychic energy from them and diffusing their patterns throughout our personalities and behaviour.

The psychic energy patterns focused in the archetypes lie at the root of Jung's attempt to explain the dynamics of telepathy and precognition. At those moments when we possess these faculties, we are experiencing, he says, not the perception of events in the outer world of objects arrayed in the fiction of space and time; rather we are in touch with something deep inside ourselves. The precognitive psyche is relating to its own extended self by way of the spaceless, timeless collective unconscious. There, attracted to some archetypal energy pattern, like atoms in solution being drawn towards a seed crystal which will gather them up and give them shape, the psyche gathers in some of the meanings (images, thoughts, scenarios of events) relevant to the emotion which first put it in touch with that particular archetype. These meanings may have come from far afield, from other centuries or other continents, but the psyche finds them bound together in the archetypal vortex, and 'in time' communicates them to its own conscious self as events 'in the future'.

Such an abstract description of the dynamics of synchronicity may be difficult to follow, but Jung illustrates it with many examples. One of the best is that of the patient whose death had apparently been foretold to his wife by the arrival of a flock of birds on the roof of their house (see p. 79). At first sight, Jung says, 'the death and the flock of birds seem to be incommensurable with one another. If one considers, however, that in the Babylonian Hades the souls wore a "feather dress", and that in ancient Egypt the *ba*, or soul was thought of as a bird, it is not too far-fetched to suppose that there may be some archetypal symbolism at work. Had such an incident occurred in a dream, that interpretation would be justified by the comparative psychological material. [37, p. 32].'

In the case of the patient who dreamt of being given a golden scarab, Jung sees another archetypal connection. This woman was, he says, stuck in her therapy and unable to get beyond a severe emotional block. The scarab dream, combined with the next day's appearance of a scarabaeid beetle in Jung's study, had the effect of breaking down her rational defences and led to a whole new phase of growth in her treatment. Relating this to the archetypes Jung says, 'Any essential change of attitude signifies a psychic renewal which is usually accompanied by symbols of rebirth in the patient's dreams and fantasies. The scarab is the classic example of a rebirth symbol. The ancient Egyptian *Book of What Is in the Netherworld* describes how the dead sun-god changes himself at the tenth station into Khepri, the scarab, and then, at the twelfth station, mounts the barge which carries the rejuvenated sun-god into the morning sky.' Thus it was the patient's strong emotional need to make a breakthrough (be 'reborn') that put her in touch with an archetypal symbol of rebirth, and then led to her apparently precognitive dream of the scarab.

Jung also felt that synchronicity could help to explain the mystery of the *I Ching*. He, no less than millions of others who have used the book successfully, had a deep respect bridging on disquiet for the 'odd fact that a reaction that makes sense arises out of a technique seemingly excluding all sense from the outset.'

How *could* the arbitrary tossing of three coins into the air produce meaningful answers to today's questions from an inscrutable collection of hexagrams written thousands of years ago? Jung's suggestion was that each of the sixty-four hexagrams in the *I Ching* represents an archetypal life situation synchronistically linked by meaning with both the moment in which the hexagram was originally cast and the moment when a latter day seeker tosses his three coins and asks for advice.

> In other words, whoever invented the *I Ching* was convinced that the hexagram worked out in a certain moment coincided wth the latter in quality no less than in time. To him the hexagram was the exponent of the moment in which it was cast – even more so than the hours of the clock or the divisions of the calender could be – inasmuch as the hexagram was understood to be an indicator of the essential situation prevailing in the moment of its origin. [34]

Thus, the meaning in a seeker's question would irresistibly be drawn to the meaning lying at the heart of the most relevant of the *I Ching*'s sixty-four hexagrams. But it is important, Jung stressed, that the *I Ching* be addressed only in moments of sincerity and with deep concentration so best to encourage the psyche's synchronistic communication with the appropriate hexagram.

Again and again Jung links synchronistic phenomena with emotion, and argues strongly for the view that people are most open to precognitive (or telepathic) awareness in states of high-pitched emotion, owing to the effect of such emotion in breaking down the threshold of normal consciousness and thus leaving the psyche more open to 'messages' from the collective unconscious. 'Every emotional state,' he writes, 'produces an alteration of consciousness . . . that is to say there is a certain narrowing of consciousness and a corresponding strengthening of the unconscious.'

Jung thought that most instances of precognition had to do with traumatic events which were accompanied by high-pitched emotion, events such as death, fatal accidents, crises, catastrophes or impending mental illness. This is certainly the case in many documented instances of spontaneous precognition, the best modern example being Barker's study of the Aberfan mining disaster; and it appears to hold for the trance states usually associated with oracles and witch doctors' prophetic gifts, but is it generally true?

On the contrary, many recorded instances of spontaneous precognition seem to forecast disarmingly trivial events. The majority of J. W. Dunne's dreams are a case in point. And in his carefully researched survey of 148 cases of spontaneous precognition, J. E. Orme noted that, 'Another characteristic feature of precognitive experiences is that relatively unimportant, even trivial, events are precognized as frequently as warnings of deaths and accidents' (54, p. 356).

There is, however, one pattern generally accepted as linking the type of high-pitched emotion which might break through the psyche's normal defences and precognitive experience. While it is true that precognitive dreams seem to be a blend of the significant and the trivial, and that such dreams make up the vast majority of reported cases of precognition, it is also true that in those cases where the premonitory experience occurs as a waking vision, it is very commonly associated with an event charged with some emotional significance.

Jung's view of a correspondence between emotional turmoil and precognitive awareness led him to join forces with the psychological camp which sees such phenomena as 'regressive'. He felt that the capacity for psychic experience was more prevalent in primitive man, with his lesser logical development and lower threshold of conscious organization, and he noted that children often show a considerable gift for experiencing ESP phenomena, which diminishes (and in most cases disappears) as they grow older.

Jung's theory of synchronicity, while mainly intuitive in its approach to explaining the dynamics of ESP, none the less marks a crucial turning point in our whole approach to the subject. He seized upon the relevance of new developments in twentieth century physics; and he was right in his view that parapsychology, if the phenomena it purports to study can be verified, makes a natural bridge between physics and psychology. Since the 1960s, it has become almost axiomatic that if a man wants to do serious work in parapsychology he has to acquaint himself with the principles of modern physics, and the more recent psychological theories on precognition mirror this awareness of their authors. We shall take a look at those theories later on. But first it is necessary to take a sideways glance at those aspects of relativity theory, quantum physics and brain physiology which have borne most directly on shaping the new trend in parapsychological thinking and research.

PART THREE

What Is Precognition?

8 Time in Relativity Theory

Albert Einstein once joked that perhaps he should have been a clockmaker. It seems a strange professional fantasy for a man whose theoretical work was to alter forever our appreciation of just how seriously we ought to treat anything a clock might choose to tell us. The publication in 1905 of his *Special Theory of Relativity* marked a radical turning point in human thought, after which many of our most basic concepts would never be the same again – and certainly not our understanding of time.

Until the beginning of this century, the common sense view of time as an ordered sequence of moments following one upon the other was very like the scientific description offered by classical physics. According to Newton, 'Absolute, true and mathematical time, of itself and from its own nature, flows equably without relation to anything external.' The same was true of space. 'Absolute space, in its own nature, without relation to anything external, remains similar and immovable . . .'

These Newtonian absolutes had dominated scientific and philosophical thinking for more than 200 years and seemed to many literally to be written into the fabric of the universe. Within such a framework, where individual events are viewed as so many steppingstones across the sands of time, it would be unthinkable to suggest that a percipient could catch a glimpse of event C. before the preceding events A and B had happened. Hence the conceptual incompatibility of precognition with both classical physics and common sense.

Einstein's revolutionary new departure was to point out that the pecking order of events in apparent sequence is not fixed and absolute; that it is, rather, merely a way of looking at things and that given a person's point of view it might be equally valid to say that C had happened before A, or that B came later than C (providing they are not causally linked). In other words, the designation of such terms as earlier or later, before or after, he said, was very often a relative matter. He arrived at this conclusion after considering the perplexing outcome of an exercise that was intended for different purposes entirely.

The now famous Michelson-Morley Experiment which set the stage for Einstein's *Special Theory of Relativity* was really intended as a 'tidying up' operation within classical physics. Since the time of early Greek science, men had believed space to be permeated by a stationary 'ether', and nineteenth-century scientists felt that this ether could be used as a frame of reference for measuring Newton's Absolute Space. Michelson and Morley set out simply to measure the strength of the 'ether wind' as the earth moved through this stationary Absolute.

They shone two beams of light at right angles, one 'into the wind' and the other 'across the wind,' fully expecting there to be a time lag between the arrivals of the two beams back at source. But no such time lag could be measured; the beams of light required exactly the same time to be reflected back to the detection plate, irrespective of the direction they had travelled. Thus, apparently, no visible effect had been exerted by the stationary ether.

Einstein then stated in his Special Relativity paper, there is no such thing as an Absolute frame of reference.

Each frame of reference, viewed from within itself, Einstein argued, is as valid as any other. Neither, he pointed out, is there any such thing as Absolute Space, nor Absolute Time. Indeed, if one is impossible so is the other because the two cannot be described separately. Movement is movement through space, and movement through space takes time. So in place of Newton's three-dimensional Absolute Space and one-dimensional Absolute Time, Einstein proffered the stunned cadres of classical physics a relativistic four-dimensional space-time continuum in which the coordinates of space and time were constantly having to be readjusted to take account of one's point of view.

The key factor in relativity theory for defining an observer's point of view is the speed at which he is travelling relative to another's point of view. According to Einstein, from the point of view of a stationary observer, a body in motion undergoes an odd triad of side-effects such that as its speed approaches the constant and inaccessible speed of light, its time processes will stretch (time slows down), the space through which it is moving will shrink, and its mass (an inverse function of this diminishing space) increase towards infinity. Given the relative nature of all motion, however, an observer riding on such a fast-moving body would remain oblivious to the distortions that others (at rest) see all around him. From his point of view, he is just sitting there while the rest of the world rushes by in a rather peculiar fashion.

Apart from its significant role in demonstrating the inadequacy of our ordinary sense of time, Einstein's *Special Theory of Relativity* has little direct bearing on thought about precognition. Since none of the reported cases discussed in earlier chapters happened to people said to be whizzing around the universe at speeds approaching that of light, the strange time distortions known to accompany such speeds cannot be thought to explain their apparently precocious access to the future. But some serious thinkers, hoping to resolve the problem of precognition, have found more relevant ideas in the *General Theory of Relativity* published eleven years later, in 1916.

Where Special Relativity restricted itself to describing the properties of bodies (or systems) travelling in a straight line at constant speed, the much more comprehensive General Theory takes into account that all objects are subject to accelerations and follow curved trajectories which are due to the presence of other masses and are commonly described as the effect of gravity. The General Theory sets out to describe the causes and effects of the universal gravitational force, and in doing so challenges our everyday notions of space and time to a degree almost beyond conception.

For our purposes, the single most important discovery to come out of General Relativity is the realization that space is curved. The influence of any mass, Einstein demonstrated, is such as to 'bend' the space in its vicinity – the amount of bending being equivalent to a gravitational field. The space around the earth is slightly curved, but the curvature is so infinitesimally small as to be nearly undetectable. The mass of the sun, however, which is significantly larger than that of the earth, is great enough to show an appreciable effect, such as is seen in the deflection of light rays coming to us from stars.

When considering the space occupied by the universe as a whole, opinions differ about the extent of the curvature. The relativity equations allow for many different solutions, each of which leads to a different cosmological model of the universe. One such model, and the most apposite one when considering precognition, was proposed by the mathematician Kurt Gödel in 1949 and suggests that there is enough mass in the universe to curve space right round on itself – such that the universe as a whole can be viewed as an enclosed, rotating sphere.*

---

*So far, the known mass in the universe is not in fact large enough to curve space to this extent, and the majority view among relativity physicists is that Gödel's model is an inaccurate description. However, assessments of universal mass are continually being revised upwards and may yet reach the critical amount suggested by Gödel. In the meantime, his model has accurately predicted certain cosmological phenomena such as black holes and it remains an important concept in the philosophy of physics.

It was demonstrated in Special Relativity that the old categories of space and time are inadequate, and in place of three-dimensional space and one-dimensional time, Einstein substituted the four-dimensional space-time continuum in which space and time were integral functions of each other. This continuum is carried over into General Relativity and thus it follows that any curvature of space requires that time, too, is curved. Thus a cosmological model like Gödel's which postulates that the universe is an enclosed, rotating sphere is also telling us that time also is curved round on itself – in other words, that time is circular. Such a formulation, of course, raises many problems for common sense and not a few for physics.

How, for instance, if time moves in a circle, do we ever speak of 'before' and 'after'? How can we ever tell which point on a circle precedes any other? In General Relativity, these 'befores' and 'afters' have no meaning. As the eminent French physicist Olivier Costa de Beauregard summed up the transformation wrought by Relativity Theory;

> In Newtonian [physics] the separation between past and future was objective, in the sense that it was determined by a single instant of universal time, the present. This is no longer true in relativistic [physics] . . . There can no longer be any objective and essential (that is, not arbitrary) division of space-time between 'events which have already occurred' and 'events which have not yet occurred'. [20, p.429]

'For us believing physicists,' said Einstein, 'this separation between past, present and future has the value of mere illusion, however tenacious.' And Costa de Beauregard added (almost as an afterthought!), 'There is inherent in this a small philosophical revolution.'

If all events are looked at within the framework of General Relativity, they become timeless phenomena in four-dimensional space-time, stretched out along the curved contour of our spherical existence as a static, changeless whole. Such a picture implies that everything that ever 'will be' now 'is', i.e., that the future is already written and is as fixed as the past.*

Graphically in such a model, the entire history of any event can be represented as a stationary curve (a 'world line'), with each 'moment

---

*There is heated controversy among theoretical physicists concerning the apparently static nature of the universe in Relativity Theory, and many argue that it need not be so – that there is, rather, scope for flux and change. Physicist David Bohm goes further than most and argues that even the past, as we know it, is not fixed.

in time' being a point on that curve, and the familiar succession of events which is part of our normal, everyday temporal perception is accounted for by the orderly movement of consciousness along such a curve. Thus, rather like passengers in a spacecraft looking out at a universe filled with events (and all their contents), we become aware of a succession of events one by one as we transit the separate points along this curve.

For precognition to be conceptually tenable in such a framework, one would only have to imagine that some people have the ability to 'jump ahead' in their perceptions, thus catching a glimpse of time from further along the stationary curve (of happenings) than most of us would normally have come to next in the ordinary course of conscious progress along the curve. Indeed, the implication that such a thing might be possible in a relativistic universe where time is laid out in a circle with no real beginning or end was suggested to Einstein by various colleagues.

Why, it was asked, could not someone jump ahead in time and then communicate back to us what he sees there? Or, alternatively, why could a man not travel backwards along the curve of events and thus revisit his own past armed with knowledge about the future? As Gödel put it, it should be perfectly possible to conceive 'certain cosmological past, present and future, and back again, exactly as it is possible in other worlds to travel to distant parts of space.'

Gödel suggested that to travel into the future we have only to fly in the direction of the universe's rotation, whereas to get into the past we fly against it. And perhaps with an amused sideways glance at Wells's *The Time Machine*, he even worked out the amount of fuel required and the velocity at which our space ship would have to travel to make such journeys – the velocity would have to be at least 70% the speed of light.

Einstein himself had always felt philosophically uncomfortable with such notions of hypothetical time travel effected by whizzing backwards and forwards along the world lines of curved space-time, and for a long time he insisted that it was impossible. 'We cannot send wire messages into the past', he declared firmly in 1928, arguing that a world line could never intersect with itself – that is, that it would never be possible to circumnavigate the universe along the the stationary curve which describes one's life in such a way as to coincide with one's own history or to overtake one's own future. The possibility of doing so, he said, would violate an essential principle of Relativity Theory – the idea that any given event can be truly simultaneous only with itself.

Yet when Gödel published his controversial solution to the relativity equations in 1949, which demonstrated that the mathematics of General Relativity do indeed allow for the possibility of self-intersecting world lines and thus the possibility that a moment 'now' can be simultaneously with another moment in the 'future' or one in the 'past', Einstein gave the paper a surprisingly sympathetic review. Perhaps, he admitted, the irreversibility of time was no longer so inviolate as he had once supposed. Modifying his previously held view about communication from the future to the past, he said:

> It is impossible to send wire messages to the past on [the level of everyday reality], but it is not necessarily true for [sub-atomic] phenomena, which seem to be reversible . . . If we concede with Gödel the possibility of the closed world-lines on the huge [cosmic] scale . . . then the relation of succession becomes relativized; for on a circular world line it is a matter of convention to say that A precedes B rather than vice versa. [20, p.437]

The possibility of time reversibility at the subatomic level was something that Einstein had grudgingly come to accept as a result of discoveries in quantum physics. We shall look at these and their implications in the next chapter. But in response to Gödel's suggestion of backwards flowing time at the cosmic level, he held out the hope that this might yet be proved wrong. 'It will be interesting,' he said, 'to weight whether these [cosmological models] are not to be excluded on physical grounds.' But events proved him wrong.

The later postulation of black holes – rotating mini-universes within our universe where the force of gravity surrounding a mass has increased to such an extent that it has pulled space-time round on itself – does provide definite physical grounds for such cosmological models, and confirms the validity of Gödel's solution for the relativity equations. And the nature of black holes as presently understood does indeed encourage speculation about travel backwards or forwards in time, albeit of a rather science-fiction sort.

Black holes are so called because the force of gravity surrounding them is so strong that once something has been sucked into one of them, it can never again get out – and this includes light rays. Thus we never see black holes, only their indirect gravitational pull on other bodies.

Just at the surface of a black hole, called its 'event horizon', gravity is so strong that time itself stands still – or so it would seem to a person on the outside looking in (or indeed to one on the inside looking out.) Thus if someone were to fall into a black hole, to those of us on the outside it would look like it had taken an infinite time for him to do so, though to him time would seem to pass normally – much the same effect predicted by relativity theory for space travellers approaching the speed of light.

The person falling into the black hole would, then, be falling into our future. If from such an inside vantage point he could communicate to us, he would indeed be 'sending wire messages to the past.' Such a scenario is portrayed by astrophysicist John Gribbin in discussing the somewhat fanciful possibility of time travel effected via flirtation with the event horizons of black holes.

> Inside a black hole, time as we know it (together with space as we know it) ceases to exist . . . [Thus] a very massive, compact object such as a black hole, with an intense gravitational field surrounding it, provides the intrepid space traveller with the means to jump into the future not just once but repeatedly . . . Just diving a spacecraft into the region of strong gravity and swinging out again on the other side, the astronaut would see time in the outside universe speeded up, with millenia – or longer intervals – flicking by in the few weeks he spent manoeuvering his spacecraft around the hole and out again [28, pp.67-8]

Of course any communication from someone inside a black hole is actually impossible, because it follows from the very definition of a black hole that nothing can escape from it – and that would include any sort of electromagnetic radiation that might carry a message. But there are further objections to getting carried away by such speculative time travel fantasies when considering the possible physics of precognition.

Communicating with people who have fallen into black holes, even were it possible, or taking round-the-universe cruises at velocities close to the speed of light, has very little to do with our ordinary earthbound experience, and figures nowhere in reported cases of alleged precognition. For all practical purposes, such possibilities might just as well be viewed alongside the wildest cogitations of a very imaginative science fiction writer, though they do have some conceptual value for the precognition theorist.

Before relativity theory and the eerie time distortions latent within it, the irreversibility of time was sacrosanct, and any suggestion of access to the future considered patently absurd. The post-Einstein intellectual climate is thus far less antipathetic to the mere possibility of precognition than was that of classical physics or common sense. It remains to be considered whether developments in quantum physics can shed more practical light on how precognition might actually function.

9   Quantum Physics: Uncertainty With No Sense of Time

For the past twenty years, parapsychologists have looked increasingly to the ideas and discoveries of quantum physics both for intellectual support and in hope of discovering some of the actual mechanisms by which psychic phenomena might function. Yet if anyone were to hope that by thus removing a faculty such as precognition from the realm of crystal balls and looking at it instead through the misty vapours of a Wilson cloud chamber* it would seem any less mysterious, he would be very sorely disappointed. Modern physics, particularly quantum physics, seems better equipped to exacerbate our sense of incredulity than to ease it.

Most writers, and indeed most physicists, find it impossible to discuss the sub-atomic processes outlined by quantum theory without falling back on adjectives like bizarre, weird, erratic and magical to describe the ghostly particles and interactions which lie just beneath the surface of our day-to-day world. Little wonder, then, that parapsychologists trying to explain disembodied thought processes and things that go bump in the night should feel a natural affinity with a branch of science that might well have been dreamt up by Lewis Carroll; but in fact the affinity runs much deeper than a shared eccentricity.

Two important physical principles have always formed the main objection to precognition from both physicists and philosophers, and both are overturned by the discoveries of quantum physics. The first is the unidirectionality of time, such that 'now' must necessarily precede 'then'. The second is causality, which states that an effect cannot precede its cause. Yet within the tiny microcosm of the atom, neither time nor causality have any meaning in the accepted sense.

In the last chapter we saw how, on the cosmological scale, relativity theory allows for the possibility of circular time and time reversibility, and thus plays havoc with the causal laws, but precognition as recorded in daily life does not happen on a cosmological scale to people

*An instrument in which the interactions of charged, sub-atomic particles can be studied by way of trails they leave in an ionized vapour.

travelling at speeds approaching that of light. Critics of any attempt to explain precognition in terms of quantum theory have argued that, equally, the erratic behaviour of sub-atomic processes has very little to do with events experienced at the level of everyday reality, but these objections are, at the very least, steeped in controversy.

As we shall see in later chapters, there is certainly evidence that the human brain is sensitive to quantum level phenomena, and precognition theorists see this sensitivity as a possible link between some quantum processes and human consciousness. In this context, there are three aspects of quantum theory worth looking at in some detail: Heisenberg's Uncertainty Principle, quantum virtual states, and quantum non-locality – or, 'action at a distance.'

The Uncertainty Principle

No man's work could bring us more directly face to face with the havoc which quantum theory has wrought in the realm of causality than that of the German physicist Werner Heisenberg. Heisenberg's proof that the foundations of our universe rest on nothing more solid than unpredictable and wholly random sub-atomic events earned him the Nobel Prize in 1931 and set fellow quantum physicists the task of completely redefining physical reality, though from Einstein it elicited the protest that such a view was, 'so very contrary to my scientific instinct that I cannot forego the search for a more complete conception' (19, p.318).

It was in direct response to the implications of Heisenberg's ideas, summed up in The Uncertainty Principle, that Einstein made his famous assertion that 'God does not play dice with the universe.' This reaction was, as it sounds, a passionately religious rather than a cool, scientific statement, yet Einstein devoted the last twenty-five years of his scientific life to an (unsuccessful) attempt to evolve a theory which would take physics beyond the rules of the gaming house.

Paradoxically, it was Einstein's own formulation that light, and all other forms of energy, comes in pre-packaged energy quanta* which led to the evolution of Heisenberg's principle. Atomic theory established that atoms consist mainly of space, with a central, massive core (the nucleus) surrounded by layers of orbiting electrons – a model which might be imagined to look something like the solar system, with

*A quantum is the most basic, indivisible unit (of energy × time) required to make any sub-atomic process happen. Any given process may require a single quantum, or many quanta – hence the name 'quantum theory'.

-124124

the nucleus in the place of the sun and electrons behaving like planets. It was an important breakthrough of quantum theory to show that each of the orbits an electron may occupy while circling the atomic nucleus represents a given energy state, and that electrons may move from one orbit to another.

But, quantum theory established, if an electron is to leave one orbit (energy state) and change to another, it must first either absorb or give off some energy, and it must do so in units of discrete quanta. And since the energy to be absorbed or radiated itself exists only in discrete units, it follows that the movements of the electrons from orbit to orbit would have to be represented as a series of discrete jumps instead of as would have been supposed in any model offered by classical physics (which held that all motion was along continuous curves).

This new description of motion as a series of discontinuous jumps was one of the most fundamental conceptual changes to come out of quantum theory. It was like replacing real life movement with the jerky, broken stages that make up the many individual frames of a moving picture film. In fact, quantum theory showed us that all movement is indeed structured like the successive presentation of frames on a film – with the added complication that, just as a film might occasionally skip a bit in the projector, so sub-atomic particles can 'jump several frames ahead,' leaving out the intermediate steps that might seem more natural.

Heisenberg's Uncertainty Principle arose from the problem of trying to follow and describe the actual movement of a sub-atomic particle along its discontinuous path. For in the course of trying, physicists found themselves up against a fundamental difficulty: quantum theory predicted that the harder one tried to scrutinize the movements of a sub-atomic particle, the more elusive it would become. Owing to the mechanics of quantum movement, the mere act of focusing on the particle would be enough to disturb it.

If, for example, a physicist wished to observe the movement of an electron around an atomic nucleus, he might try to locate it under a very high-powered microscope. But vision depends upon the transmission of light from an object to the eye, so in order to produce such a transmission, he would have to focus at least one photon of 'light'* on to the electron. But a photon of light is a quantum of energy,

*In fact, as Heisenberg pointed out, it would have to be a beam of gamma rays rather than light waves, because even the highest frequency of visible light would have too long a wavelength to detect an electron.

and when it strikes the electron it will disturb it, causing it to change its direction and speed – its momentum.

Hoping to get around this problem of disturbing the electron's momentum, the physicist might then try focusing light of a lower frequency on to the electron. As Einstein demonstrated, the frequency of any radiation is directly proportional to the amount of energy it carries, so lower frequency light would carry less energy and thus be less likely to unsettle the electron. But as soon as he tries this, the physicist has a different problem. He finds that his low frequency light won't make a distinct image. A low frequency light wave would have a very long wavelength, and thus it would produce a fuzzy, approximate picture that left it unclear just *where* the electron is.

So the physicist hoping to measure the movement of an electron would find himself in the position of having to choose between knowing its momentum while blurring its position, or of knowing its position while disturbing its momentum – he can never know both, though both would be necessary if he were ever to say anything meaningful about the electron's movement. And that is the nub of the Uncertainty Principle: that at a certain level of reality we come up against a barrier beyond which it is impossible ever to make a full set of exact measurements, and hence impossible ever to *know* exactly just how the constituents of matter are behaving.

According to Heisenberg, this uncertainty is a built-in feature of the universe and not just a drawback associated with our having to use clumsy instruments. In describing the motions of particles, he said, we would always have to content ourselves with approximations. Given a long enough 'run' of measurements, the approximations would, following the laws of probability, form some sort of picture, but this picture would be the result of a statistical trend rather than an exact, objective description of any one electron's movement.

As Heisenberg's colleague Max Born expressed it, 'Physics is in the nature of the case indeterminate, and therefore the affair of statistics' (8, p.102). But that is not the worst of it. Drawing out the implications of this indeterminacy, Born goes on to say,

> . . . if we can never actually determine more than one of the two properties [of a particle] (possession of a definite position and of a definite momentum), and if when one is determined we can make no assertion at all about the other property for the same moment, so far as our experiment goes, then we are not justified in concluding that the 'thing' under examination can actually be described as a particle in the usual sense of the term. [8, p.97]

But if an electron is not a particle 'in the usual sense,' what is it? The question brings us face to face with another revolutionary discovery of quantum physics: that matter itself is not necessarily material in the ordinary sense of that word. Rather, at the sub-atomic level at least, matter has a dual nature such that elementary particles can be described with equal validity as behaving either like waves or like particles.

If, for example, an electron collides with another electron, it does behave like a particle, and the collision of two such particles would leave familiar trails in a Wilson cloud chamber. But if an electron is fired at a screen containing two slits, instead of choosing to pass through one or the other as a particle would have to, it suddenly takes on the properties of a wave, passes through both slits, *and* interferes with itself!

'Elementary particles,' said Sir William Bragg, 'seem to be waves on Mondays, Wednesdays and Fridays, and particles on Tuesdays, Thursdays and Saturdays' (38, p. 52). In short, we can never be really sure when or under what circumstances an electron (or any other sub-atomic 'particle') will behave as a wave or when as a particle,* and thus quantum physicists have given up the over-simplistic either (particle)/or (wave) mode of description and speak instead of 'matter-waves'.

Matter-waves are complex mathematical entities that express both possible manifestations of the electron's dualistic nature (and, indeed, all of its other possible properties, such as its position or its energy state), and they represent quantum theory's compromise solution to the problem of how to describe a reality that recedes from focus whenever we try to look at it.

Under the 'Principle of Complementarity,' quantum theory states that while we can never be sure whether we are dealing with an electron in its wave or in its particle form, the two possibilities taken together complement each other in such a way that we can at least describe the motions and interactions of the 'package deal' (the matter-wave) – thus getting an *approximate* picture of reality. But that approximate picture – and this is the cutting edge of quantum theory which outraged Einstein's sensibilities – is never more than a distribution of the probabilities that, under any given set of circumstances, the matter-wave will express itself in this way or in that,

*Though in choosing our experiments we do determine which identity the electron will manifest *as we measure it* – thus a quantum physicist's observation of an event helps to determine that which he observes!

and until it does so, *reality itself* (the reality of that electron) must be said to consist of probabilities. In fact, matter-waves are generally referred to as 'probability waves'.

Drawing out the full implications of Heisenberg's Uncertainty Principle then, it is fair to say that, according to quantum theory, reality at its most primary level consists not of any fixed actualities that we *can* know but rather of all the probabilities of the various fixed actualities that we *might* know. Clearly some proportion of these probabilities do at some stage become actualities, to which the world of our everyday experience bears adequate witness, but how? At what stage, and why, does one or another of nature's manifold possibilities fix itself in the world of 'real things,' and what role is played by all the 'lost probabilities' in achieving this final state of affairs?

Virtual States

In fact, it is because quantum theory demonstrates that there are not, and never can be, any good answers to most of these last few questions that it has represented such an effective assault on the time-honoured laws of causality.

When the classical notion of continuous motion over a definite path was replaced by the quantum view of jerky transitions from one energy state to another via discrete quantum leaps, the breach was opened. For it soon became clear that if an atomic system is disturbed (either internally or externally), the resulting electron transitions occur in a completely random way.

A transition may occur, for instance, at any time and without any attributable cause. Suddenly,* without any prior warning, rhyme or reason, a previously 'quiet' atom may experience chaos in its electron energy shells, and we can never predict when this will happen to any particular atom. It's just a matter of chance. Further – and this is why there is said to be time reversibility at the quantum level – an electron might, with equal probability, make a transition from a higher energy state to a lower one, or from a lower energy state to a higher one (7, p.415).

Thus in no familiar sense can we speak of a 'succession of events' amongst quantum phenomena, as though one thing had led necessarily to another. It would be accurate to say that one event was

---

*The whole process of electron transitions within an excited atom takes only a few micro-micro-seconds, so any 'suddenly' in our everyday world is a very long time indeed by comparison.

related to another, but quite wrong to describe one as a cause and the other as an effect. They just 'happen as they happen'. And worse still, which brings us to the question of the 'lost probabilities,' during the early stages of its being disturbed, the electron transitions occurring within an excited atomic system *occur simultaneously in all directions at once*. That is, an excited electron behaves as though 'it were smeared out over a large region of space' (13, p. 128).

If, for example, an electron is struck by a photon, it will have picked up energy from the photon and thus can no longer carry on happily circling round the nucleus in the orbit it had been occupying so stably. It must instead go off in search of some new orbit more suited to its newly excited state. But given that nothing is determined in quantum physics, there are *many* new orbits where it might possibly settle down. While only a proportion of these would offer the electron a stable, permanent* home, how is it to know which one unless it tries them all? And that is exactly what it does.

An excited electron, in the guise of a probability wave, puts out 'feelers', during the course of which it simultaneously situates itself, temporarily, in *all* of its possible new homes. And until such time as it registers itself as living at some permanent address, it *really is* living at all of its temporary ones.

In quantum theory, these 'temporary addresses' are referred to as 'virtual transitions', while the final, 'permanent address' is called a 'real transition'. However, as quantum physicist David Bohm cautions, we must not be misled by the use of such terms as 'real' and 'virtual':

> Sometimes permanent (i.e., energy-conserving) transitions are called *real* transitions, to distinguish them from the so-called *virtual* transitions, which do not conserve energy and which must therefore reverse before they have gone too far. This terminology is unfortunate, because it implies that virtual transitions have no real effects. On the contrary, they are often of the greatest importance, for a great many physical processes are the result of these so-called *virtual* transitions. [7, p.415]

The situation is a bit like that of someone from modest circumstances who has just won the pools. His new-found wealth, he feels, makes it unsuitable that he should go on living in his simple two-bedroomed flat on the same street where he was born. A whole world of new

---

*Ultimately, the electron will return to the shell it was occupying before its system became excited, because that shell is its *most* energy conserving position, but there are several semi-'permanent' shells where it might rest along the way.

possibilities has opened to him, and he wants to realize his greatest potential for ownership of his dream home. In the 'real world' (the world of everyday reality), of course, he would have to explore these possibilities one by one, perhaps moving house eight or ten times before feeling certain he had found just the right one.

But in the quantum world, the winner would simply take up residence in *all* of his possible new houses, *all at once*. If his stockbroker wished to pin him down in order to post him a dividend cheque, he would find it an impossible task (since he really is at all of these addresses) and would just have to send duplicates to each of the houses. And if these houses were close enough to one another,* the winner could even stand on each of his various doorsteps and wave at himself.

In the end, of course, having explored his various possibilities to the full, the winner would settle down permanently in one house, but not without having left 'traces' of himself in the various neighbourhoods where he had temporarily occupied houses. The neighbours might remember seeing him and wonder, 'Whatever happened to that man who left so suddenly?' Some of them might even have changed their own habits as a result of living next door to the winner during his temporary stay. ('. . . For a great many physical processes are the result of these *virtual* transitions.')

While the case of the quantum world pools winner may seem somewhat far-fetched, we need look no further than biological evolution to see real life results of something very much like quantum virtual transitions. As Bohm, among others, suggests, 'in many ways, the concept of a virtual transition resembles the idea of evolution in biology, which states that all kinds of species can appear as a result of mutations, but that only certain species can survive indefinitely, namely, those satisfying certain requirements for survival in the specific enviroment surrounding the species'. (7, p.414)

The many species which are suddenly thrown up by way of mutations can be viewed as various possibilities (virtual states) being explored by Nature as new ways through which she might express her potential. The less viable possibilities do, as Bohm says, eventually fall by the wayside, but often not without first leaving some trace of themselves which goes on to become part of life's fabric. Two doomed mutations might, for instance, before dying out, cross-breed to form some third mutation which is quite able to survive indefinitely (a real

---

*In fact, in quantum physics it would make no difference how far apart the houses were, because a particle's virtual transitions can interfere with each other over any distance.

transition). This is most likely the way that the human species came about, a successful secondary mutation of some shadowy life form referred to only as 'the missing link'.

Non-Locality, or 'Action-at-a-Distance'

It is in direct consequence of the significance of virtual states, whereby the wave function of an elementary particle is 'smeared out over a large region of space,' that quantum theory makes its boldest and most revolutionary prediction – that is, that there can be connections and correlations between very distant events *in the absence of any intermediary force or signal*, and that such 'action-at-a-distance' will be *instantaneous*.

This 'Principle of Non-Locality' (that something can be affected in the absence of any local cause) is highlighted in Bell's Theorem, and it follows necessarily from the fundamentally indeterminate nature of reality as suggested by the wave equations of quantum theory.

Quantum theory indicates that there are no such things as separate parts in reality, but instead only intimately related phenomena so bound up with each other as to be inseparable. This view holds that our physical world is, '. . . not a structure built out of independently existing unanalysable entities, but rather a web of relationships between elements whose meanings arise wholly from their relationships to the whole' (70).

Such a vision, with its obviously mystical overtones, flies directly in the face not only of common sense and classical physics but also of relativity theory – all of which rest on the intuitive principle that the bits out of which reality is composed are inherently separate and that any witnessed affect on one bit has an assignable cause from some other bit, mediated by way of some locally detectable force or signal.

Einstein added a further element to this doctrine of 'local causes' by stating that no signal could travel from one bit of reality (a cause) to another (its effect) faster than light, and thus he could have no truck with quantum theory's assertion that an influence could be instantaneous. Indeed, it was because of its championing of instantaneous 'action-at-a-distance' that Einstein insisted quantum theory had to be an incomplete description of reality, and he set out to illustrate this in the famous Einstein, Podolsky, Rosen Paradox – the EPR Paradox, published in 1935.

The gist of the EPR Paradox* can be understood by imagining the fortunes of a hypothetical set of twins**, born in London but separated since birth, with one twin still living in London and the other resident in New York. The twins have never met one another, indeed neither even knows he has a twin, and there has never been any form of communication between them. On the commonsense view of things, then, they have led entirely separate lives. Yet despite this ignorance and lack of communication, a psychologist studying the twins has noted an amazing similarity in their behaviour and circumstances. Each twin has adopted the nickname 'Scotty', each chose to join the police force and rose to the rank of Detective Inspector, each dresses almost exclusively in blue, each was married in the same year to a brunette named Mary, etc. How do we explain all this?

The quantum theorist would have no problem with such apparently inexplicable correlations between the lives of the twins, because his equations had always led him to expect it, and so long as his mathematical predictions come true, he doesn't much care why. But Einstein could not leave it at that, and he felt the quantum theorist's willingness to do so was proof of the incompleteness of quantum theory.

In the first place, Einstein could not abandon his belief (already upset by the Uncertainty Principle) that a complete physical theory *should* be able to explain the 'Why?' of things and say something definite about the nature of reality; and secondly, he could not accept that there was not some 'law-abiding' explanation underlying any observed correlations between the obviously separate lives of the twins.

> One can escape from this conclusion [that quantum theory is incomplete] only by assuming that either the measurement of S^1 [one twin] *telepathically* changes the real situation of S^2 [the other twin], or by denying independently real situations [lives] as such to things which are spatially separated from each other. Both alternatives appear to me entirely unacceptable. [18, p.85]

So, to avoid falling back on either telepathy or the possibility of some

---

*The EPR Paradox itself relates to a thought experiment proposed by Einstein, Podolsky and Rosen in which a physicist would hope to measure the positions and momenta of two protons as they flew off in opposite directions from a common source. David Bohm later revised this by suggesting the physicist measure the spin on two protons, and Bohm's suggestion became the basis for the real correlation experiments carried out in the 70's.

**This twins example for illustrating the EPR paradox is the author's own.

mysterious connection between distant situations, Einstein proposed his third way out – that there was some common factor in the very nature of the situations that would account for their correlated behaviour.

In our example of the twins, this common factor could be illustrated by our saying they must be *identical* twins, with shared genetic material. Einstein would say, then, that if the twins' lives run along similar lines as predicted by quantum theory, this was simply because they were programmed to do so from the beginning by that common genetic factor deep within their natures. Thus there is no telepathy and no mysterious 'action-at-a-distance' in their similar lifestyles, but rather a common factor that quantum theory must fail to take into account because of its refusal to make any statements about the nature of underlying reality.*

For many years Einstein's proposed proof that quantum theory is incomplete lay side by side in a state of near oblivion with the predictions of non-locality. Those few physicists who thought about the EPR Paradox at all thought that at least the 'common factor' (hidden variables) solution would be compatible with any predictions of quantum theory, and thus it seemed in some ways academic whether Einstein was right in saying that these predictions could be explained with reference to an underlying reality. But all this was changed by the publication of Bell's Theorem in 1964.

Bell, a physicist at the CERN laboratories in Geneva, proved mathematically that *either* Einstein was right, that there is a fundamental reality in the physical world underlying the indeterminacy of quantum physics, and thus quantum theory is wrong, *or* Einstein himself was all wrong to suppose there is an underlying reality, and quantum theory is correct in predicting genuine action-at-a-distance. Bell asserted his definite either/or on the basis of a proof that Einstein's idea and the quantum theory would lead not to the same predictions in a certain experimental situation**, as had been thought, but to entirely different ones. Though Bell's Theorem itself is highly mathematical, it can be expressed through the example of the twins.

---

*Einstein's suggestion of a common factor underlying the correlation effects predicted by quantum theory is known as the Theory of Hidden Variables.
**Ironically, the experimental situation which Bell proved would settle the issue was David Bohm's variation on the original EPR thought experiment. Thus Einstein was to be hoisted on his own petard.

Suppose the psychologist observing the twins has noticed that both are accident prone. Each was injured playing football at the age of 16, each smashed his car at the age of 25, etc. Now in a situation like this, Einstein would assert that accident-proneness must be an inherited trait and that the twins' respective brushes with bad fortune were programmed to happen. The quantum theorist would say that he knows nothing about genetics, but his equations show that if an accident befalls one twin, then a similar accident must befall the other as well. What Bell did was to prove that there is one kind of accident which would demonstrate once and for all whether the twins' accident proneness was indeed an inherited trait.

Effectively, Bell suggested that the twin living in New York should be *pushed* down a flight of stairs so that he would break a leg. Now since no one would argue that someone could inherit a tendency to be pushed downstairs by an unfriendly stranger, if a similar accident happened to the twin living in London, Einstein could not possibly argue that it did so because of any common genetic pool. If both twins fell down a flight of stairs at the same time (only the one in New York having been pushed by us) and each ended up with a broken leg, then there would *have* to be some sort of telepathy of 'action-at-a-distance' operating between them. Quantum theory would be vindicated.

If, on the other hand, the twin living in London continued to walk about safely on both legs while the twin in New York was having his broken leg set in a cast, then Einstein would be proved right. He could say that all previously noted similarities were based on inherited characteristics (hidden variables), and in situations not covered by inheritied characteristics, one wouldn't expect to find similarities (correlations).

In fact, the alternatives outlined in Bell's theorem were tested in the laboratory in 1974 when two Berkeley physicists, Stuart Freedman and John Clauser, managed to complete a successful correlation experiment on polarized photons. Freedman and Clauser established beyond doubt that the mysterious correlations do happen as quantum theory predicts,* and their ability to do so by registering macroscopic effects (i.e., effects visible on the everyday level of reality) on their

---

*The Freedman & Clauser experiment has been repeated successfully several times since, though as yet no one has been able to carry out a further and more difficult experiment to establish that the correlations are indeed instantaneous – i.e., happening at faster than the speed of light. Alain Aspect of the Optics Institute at the University of Paris is working on such a superluminary experiment.

laboratory apparatus goes further – to show that Bell's theorem and 'action-at-a-distance' have implications well beyond the sub-atomic level of reality. As one quantum physicist puts it,

> The important thing about Bell's theorem is that it puts the dilemma posed by quantum phenomena clearly into the realm of macroscopic (everyday level) phenomena . . . [and] shows that our ordinary ideas about the world are somehow profoundly deficient even on the macroscopic level [70].

In his study of Special Relativity, David Bohm makes much the same point about the conceptual challenges of relativistic physics, suggesting that where relativistic concepts of space and time clash with our common sense perception of the world, it may be that that clash is owing to our everyday perceptions being based on 'our limited and inadequate understanding of the *domain of common experience*, rather than because of any inherent inevitability in our habitual mode of apprehending this domain' (6, p.187).

Thus it would appear that one frequently expressed objection levelled by opponents of parapsychology to drawing any parallels between the strange goings-on of quantum physics and the equally strange happenings of psychic research – that sub-atomic events bear no relation to the way things happen in the everyday (macroscopic) world – is not necessarily valid. In the wake of Bell's theorem, we now know that it is at least *theoretically* possible to look towards relevant quantum phenomena when attempting to explain any proven psychic phenomena which researchers might produce.

Interestingly enough, the hypothetical example of the twins used here to illustrate quantum level correlation effects and Bell's theorem might itself be very close to a *real* example of macroscopic 'action-at-a-distance', or telepathy. In recent years psychologists studying sets of identical twins who have been separated since birth have noted the kind of uncanny correlations mentioned in the hypothetical case – the adoption of similar hairstyles and clothes preferences, similar occupations, marriages at roughly similar times to similar spouses, etc. And naturally this has led to speculation about how many such similarities can be explained by the genetic tie, and how many ought perhaps to be put down to some sort of telepathy. Only one such study has introduced a factor similar to the challenge of Bell's theorem – a nasty accident happening to one twin and its effect or lack of it on the other.

A quartet of Japanese psychologists did a depth study of three pairs of identical twins. In each pair, one twin had been exposed to the atomic bomb, and the other had not. Social and psychological studies conducted on the twins years after the war showed remarkable similarity in lifestyle, income, basic personality and family relationships, though in each set the twin exposed to the bomb showed a higher level of anxiety in response to certain Rorschach colour tests, and the unexposed twin showed little understanding of this (79). This mixture of similarities and dissimilarities is somewhat inconclusive, and the test sample is very small, but it points the way towards further research which might establish the existence or non-existence of telepathic ties between twins. The Japanese results themselves must be interpreted as a slightly negative indication.

'Action-at-a-Temporal-Distance'

Although Bell's theorem and the non-locality experiments of Freedman and Clauser might have very great implications for telepathy, it could be argued that they bear little direct relation to the problem of precognition. The Freedman and Clauser experiments refer to two events happening *at the same time but in different places*, whereas the key factor in precognition is that two events happening at *different times* (one of them still in the future) seem to have an effect on each other.

There is however, a – strangely, less talked about – set of experiments conducted by Rochester Universary physicists R. L. Pfleegor and L. Mandel in 1967 which demonstrate exactly this effect – a non-local correlation between two events happening *in the same place, but at different times*.

The Pfleegor and Mandel experiment*, like that of Freedman and Clauser, works with photons, and its implications are drawn out in extremely complex mathematical language; but again, the jist of the experiment can be summed up in an analogy.

Suppose that there are two office clerks who work in the same office, but one (A) comes in for the morning shift and the other (B) comes in for the afternoon. Just outside the office door there are two coathooks reserved for the use of A and B.

Until recently, A and B had always worked on the same shift, and

---

*Basically, the experiment consists of displaying and analysing interference effects between two low intensity photon beams emitted by two separate lasers, and results in showing there is an interference effect in the target area when only one photon is present at any given time.

when they did so, it was noticed that it was entirely random who used which coathook. Thus neither had established any pattern of using one coathook or the other. Now, when they began working separate shifts, this randomness in selecting which coathook to use persisted – but with a crucial difference. When A arrived for his morning shift, he would randomly select one of the two coathooks; when B arrived for the afternoon shift, he would always use whichever coathook A had not used. Thus, though A and B were now arriving for work at different times, they continued to hang their coats in a way that suggested both were present. Their behaviour was uncannily linked across any intervening time gap, so as always to be correlated.

The correlations demonstrated in the Pfleegor and Mandel experiment were always so exactly symmetrical that it would make no sense to say A chose one particular coathook in anticipation of B choosing the other, or that B chose his because of some telepathic awareness of which one A had chosen earlier. All that one can say is that they showed how two events can be somehow related across time in a way that ensures they will always be correlated, and any attempt to set up a cause and effect relationship between them would be meaningless.

Thus in the kind of non-local, 'action-at-a-distance' relationships which occur in quantum physics, neither space nor time exists in the ordinary sense of 'a distance between places' or a 'distance between moments'. In the Freedman and Clauser experiment which tested the alternatives of Bell's theorem, the photons behaved as though they were 'smeared out over a large region of space'; in the Pfleegor and Mandel experiment, they behaved as though they were smeared out over a large region of time. In each case, distance is replaced by relationship.

It follows from this that if precognition were seen as a macroscopic manifestation of the kind of non-local time effects demonstrated by Pfleegor and Mandel, there would no longer be any grounds for saying it raises a philosophical paradox about causality. Where distance, both spatial and temporal, is replaced by relationship, cause and effect no longer have any meaning. It also follows that with such a model, any objections that precognition would imply the impossibility of free will would also have to be seen in a new light – but they will be discussed in Chapter Twelve.

10   Consciousness and Quantum Phenomena

For anyone seriously seeking a physical explanation for psychic phenomena, quantum theory clearly holds out many tantalizing prospects. In broad conceptual terms, at least, most of the once apparently insurmountable philosophic and material objections to the mere possibility of things like psychokinesis, telepathy and precognition have been overturned by the new physics.

The Principle of Complementarity established that matter and energy are two sides of the same coin, and if, as seems likely, consciousness itself is some sort of mental energy, then it no longer seems so far-fetched to consider that the mind might be able to exert some influence on matter (psychokinesis). This view is strengthened further by the way that quantum theory has removed any hard and fast distinction between the observer and the observed in demonstrating that consciousness apparently plays an active role in determining the outcome of any experiments conducted to study quantum phenomena.* And the experiments on Bell's theorem have established that strange, acausal influences transcending the limitations of both distance and time somehow link elementary particles on the quantum level of reality in a manner suggestive of the mind's apparent ability to transcend distance (telepathy) or time (precognition) on the macroscopic level.

But if any of these very promising quantum effects is to be considered as directly relevant in explaining the actual mechanics of something like precognition, then it is not enough to point out that they happen between elementary particles reacting in a vacuum under laboratory conditions. Some evidence must be found that there is a natural bridge between quantum phenomena and human consciousness, so that our everyday thoughts and perceptions might be influenced by the strange

*The apparent role of consciousness in collapsing the wave function of an elementary particle is discussed further on pp. 150–152 where it forms the basis of one of the dominant theories about how precognition works.

behaviour of elementary particles. And the crucial question here is whether there is any known mechanism in the brain, such that our awareness of events in the world might be at least partially formed in response to quantum level phenomena – and especially in response to quantum indeterminacy.

Quantum Indeterminacy in the Brain

The human brain consists, essentially, of ten thousand million (10^{10}) nerve cells called 'neurones', and these neurones, like nerve cells anywhere else in the body, are sensitive to stimulation from outside influences. The brain is often compared to a computer because there is some similarity between the complexity of the way its bundles of neurones are organized and the spaghetti of wiring which makes up the electrical circuitry of a computer.

Like the 'nerve cells' of a computer, the brain's neurones, too, are a form of electrical wiring, with the various messages that pass into and out of the brain doing so by way of electrochemical pulses flowing along the neurones. And just as the electrical wiring in a machine works more, or less, efficiently depending on the conductivity of the wiring and the strength of the electrical pulses transmitted along the wiring, so the neurones in the brain pass on more, or less, information depending on the conductivity of the neurone itself and the strength of the stimulus hitting the neurone.

In living tissue, the chemical concentrations (of hormones, metabolites, drugs, salts, etc.) surrounding the junctions (synapses) between neurones determine how effectively they will conduct electrical pulses, and hence information. If a neurone is surrounded by a weak chemical concentration of certain key substances, it will require a very large electrical input to stimulate it into action; if the surrounding chemical concentration is strong, then the neurone will 'fire' under the influence of a much weaker electrical input. The amount of electrical stimulation required to make a neurone fire (i.e., respond to stimulation and pass on some information) is called its 'stimulation threshold'.

In the ordinary course of perception, neurones are being excited at or beyond their stimulation thresholds all the time by the very strong electrical impulses generated by the surrounding environment. We see because light rays stimulate optical neurones, we hear because sound waves stimulate auditory neurones, and so on. But the question which bears on the brain's ability to react to quantum level phenomena is whether a quantum process would generate a large enough electrical pulse to fire neurones by exciting them at the minimum level of their stimulation thresholds.

In fact, it has been known for decades that the visual cortex of the human brain is sensitive enough to register a single photon of light, and that is equivalent to saying that it is registering a single quantum process – the passage of one electron from a higher energy state within an atom to a lower energy state. Such single quantum processes are, of course, subject to the Uncertainty Principle, and are the locus for the kind of non-local effects discussed in the last chapter. Before settling finally into its most stable state (and thereby emitting a photon), the electron is spread out through space and time in a myriad virtual transitions, interfering with itself and with other electrons in flagrant disregard of causality or temporality.

Whether the brain can tune into that shadowy realm of virtual transitions remains the 'sixty-four thousand dollar question' of precognition theorists,* but experiments conducted as early as the 1940s established that single cortical (brain) neurones are subject to an Uncertainty Principle of their own and that quantum indeterminacy is built into the functioning of the brain itself – through random variations in the chemical concentrations surrounding the neurone synapses.

As indicated by the fact that a single photon (quantum of light) will excite the optic nerve, the synapses of neurones are so tiny and so sensitive that the likelihood of their firing (their stimulation threshold) varies according to quantum fluctuations in the surrounding ionic fluid. As these fluctuations are wholly random, it is no more possible to say just when any one neurone will fire than it is possible to predict when any one electron will become excited. Laboratory tests on isolated neurones prove that their stimulation thresholds vary according to definite statistical law, just like any other quantum process.

Not all cortical neurones are subject to quantum indeterminacy. Only those which are stimulated at or near their stimulation thresholds will be sensitive to the quantum level excitation of the surrounding fluids. If the stimulation comes in at a higher level, as it does in normal perception, then it will drown out the much more delicate, quantum

---

*The possible relationship between precognition and quantum virtual states will be discussed in the next chapter.

level stimuli. But of the 10^{10} neurones thought to exist in the brain, experimental data suggests that about 10^7 are at any time being stimulated at or near the marginal threshold for quantum sensitivity (47, p.271). In contrast, there are approximately 10^6 neurones in the optic nerve – thus the quantum level input to the brain is at least ten times as large as the visual input.

In states of reduced brain activity, such as during sleep or in meditative or trance states, the proportion of neurones subject to marginal stimulation is increased – thus increasing the susceptibility to stimulation by quantum indeterminate phenomena in those states. Interestingly enough, it is also in such relaxed states that a preponderance of alpha waves is recorded on EEG patterns, and as was discussed earlier (p. 100), alpha waves may well be associated with enhanced ESP ability.

Quantum Indeterminacy and Conscious Thought

So far, we have been discussing the sensitivity of single cortical neurones to microscopic quantum indeterminacy, and all that has been said is established scientific fact. There is no doubt that at that most basic level, the constituent elements of the brain are affected by quantum processes. However, while it may be encouraging to find *any* element of brain functioning which is turned into quantum phenomena, the isolated behaviour of single neurones is still a very long way from the coherent (synchronous) firing patterns of millions of neurones that go to make up our ordinary conscious awareness. And whether this macroscopic coherence (manifested as conscious awareness) has any quantum mechanical foundation is still purely a matter of speculation – though nearly all physical theories of precognition would require that it exists.

Coherent brain *waves* certainly exist, as frequently demonstrated on EEG patterns, and the higher the level of consciousness being monitored, the greater is the spread of such coherence. Thus a brain in deep sleep registers very few coherent brain waves; a brain engaged in ordinary waking activity, a few more; a brain concentrating very hard on some creative task, more still; and a brain engaged in something like transcendental meditation the highest level of coherence of all. EEG studies of Einstein's brain showed a consistent pattern of coherent alpha waves most of the time!

But coherent brain waves, for all their tantalizing links with higher consciousness, are produced at the neurone level, by millions of neurones reacting in phase, and there is no proven link between this kind of (macroscopic) coherence and the (microscopic) coherence of quantum wave functions found in such phenomena as superfluidity or superconductivity. None the less, some quantum physicists interested in working out the physics of consciousness speculate that something like superconductivity may prove to be the underlying basis of conscious processes, and many believe that the many similarities between conscious processes and quantum mechanical processes are too uncanny to be mere coincidence. As David Bohm puts it,

> We may well now ask whether the close analogy between quantum processes and our inner experiences and thought processes is mere coincidence . . . the remarkable point-by-point analogy between the thought processes and quantum processes would suggest that a hypothesis relating these two may well turn out to be fruitful. If such a hypothesis could ever be verified, it would explain in a natural way a great many features of our thinking. [7, pp.170–1]

The analogy between thought processes and quantum processes which Bohm had in mind was threefold, and drew a parallel between the Uncertainty Principle and certain aspects of consciousness.

The central tenet of the Uncertainty Principle is that it is impossible ever to pin down a quantum event with great precision, because the mere act of looking at it (attempting to measure its position and its momentum) changes what one was hoping to see. Bohm points out that the same is true of thought. 'If a person tries to observe what he is thinking about at the very moment that he is reflecting on a particular subject, it is generally agreed that he introduces unpredictable and uncontrollable changes in the way his thoughts proceed thereafter' (7, p.169).

Secondly, the non-local relationships which follow from the Uncertainty Principle imply that different aspects of a quantum process cannot be broken down into separate bits affecting each other via the causal laws, but rather the whole system must be seen in terms of its indivisible, inner connectedness, each part making sense only in terms of the whole. So too with thought: '. . . the significance of thought processes appears to have indivisibility of a sort. Thus, if a person attempts to apply to his thinking more and more precisely defined elements, he eventually reaches a stage where further analysis cannot even be given a meaning. Part of the significance of each element of a thought process appears, therefore, to originate in its indivisible and incompletely controllable connections with other elements' (7, p.169).

Finally, Bohm draws a parallel between the role that classical concepts play in making it possible to describe the everyday world of separate objects and causal relationships which overlay and are the limit of quantum processes, and the role that logical concepts play in structuring the 'indeterminate', flowing nature of thought processes. 'Without the development of logical thinking, we would have no clear way to express the results of our thinking, and no way to check its validity. Thus, just as life as we know it would be impossible if quantum theory did not have its present classical limit, thought as we know it would be impossible unless we could express its results in logical terms' (7, p.170).

In addition to these analogies between thought processes and quantum indeterminacy mentioned by Bohm, there is at least one further one which is particularly relevant to the theme of precognition: a parallel between the role of fantasy in psychological development and the role of virtual transitions in the evolution of quantum processes.

The mechanism of fantasy seems designed for us to throw out 'feelers' towards the future. Temporarily, in our minds, we live out a possible future situation to see whether it suits us or not. Some fantasies seem so far fetched as to be very improbable ('What would I do if I won the pools next week?'), and thus fall by the wayside. Others are quite possible, thus more probable ('Next Saturday I may go swimming, I may play tennis, I may visit a friend . . .') and more likely to condense into actual future behaviour.

In children, particularly, such future-oriented fantasies are important as a way the child can test the waters of his adult prospects. He lives out being a cowboy, a fireman, a doctor, etc., and very commonly has conversations between his various fantasy selves – a correlate of the interference patterns which can be observed when probability waves of the same elementary particle intersect.

In summary, then, there is no shortage of good analogies between the mechanics of thought and the mechanics of quantum processes, and these are among the many tantalizing reasons to suppose that consciousness itself is most likely a quantum phenomenon. Yet it is still the case that that crucial link is missing which would demonstrate how isolated microscopic quantum events (resulting in the firing of individual neurones) could be amplified to produce macroscopic quantum coherence. In the absence of some such mechanism, the link between quantum theory and consciousness must remain hypothetical. But, as Bohm says, 'If it should be true that the thought processes depend critically on quantum-mechanical elements in the brain, then we could say that thought processes provide the same kind of direct experience of the effects of quantum theory that muscular forces provide for classical theory' (7, p.171). Most of the theories that follow work on the basis of this hypothesis.

11   Physical Theories of Precognition

We left off attempting to understand how precognition might actually work after looking at Jung's Theory of Synchronicity in Chapter Seven. Jung himself had got far enough to see that developments in relativity theory and quantum physics had to be considered in any attempt to explain precognition, though his own effort to do so was mainly intuitive. Nevertheless, Jung was the first to highlight the very important question of whether the laws of the new physics couldn't be applied to the realm of human consciousness in a way that would explain psychic phenomena, and that question itself represented a major innovation in traditional ways of thinking about the subject. Most of the physical theories of precognition offered since have followed on where Jung left off.

In trying to understand the actual mechanics of precognition, there are really two separate questions to be dealt with, and the success of any physical theory must be judged by its ability to give satisfactory answers to both questions.

First, how, in terms of current physical theories, can we make sense of the future already being there, so that there is even the possibility of access to it?

Secondly, once we understand what it might mean that the future does in some way exist now, by what *means* might we have access to it – i.e., to what physical mechanism in our brains might we attribute precognitive awareness?

Nature of the Precognized Event

In attempting to answer the first question, it is important to get clear just what precognition is a precognition *of*. The gift of foresight, if it is genuine, implies that, in some sense, some aspects of the future must exist 'now'. If there are people who actually see events unfolding before they have happened, then it follows that there must be *something* there which they are seeing. The nature of that something, though, is open to two different interpretations, each embodying its own notion of time, and each suggesting its own theories of how precognition actually works.

On the first interpretation, the event seen in the precognitive experience is thought to be an *actual event* which has taken place, or which definitely will take place, though so far as human consciousness is concerned it is still 'yet to happen'. This suggests a view of time in which the future is already fully played out, or at least written. The cast, the scenes and all the actions which comprise the future are already there now (or at least simply waiting in the wings), if only we have the eye to see them.

This view of the precognized event is the traditional one, and the notion of time embodied in it is no embarrassment to modern physics. As already discussed (see Chapter Eight p. 118), it is perfectly compatible with General Relativity and Einstein's notion of a static four-dimensional space-time continuum.

On the second interpretation of the actual contents of a precognitive vision, the something which is precognized is not an *actual* future event, but rather someone's *future perception* of a *possible* future event. This at first sight slightly tortuous concept suggests that someone apparently experiencing prevision is in fact foreseeing the future state of his own mind – i.e., that he has somehow managed to make telepathic contact with a future manifestation of himself and thus see 'now' what his future self might be perceiving 'then'. The emphasis is not on what *will be*, but rather on what *may be seen*. It does not imply that the future is already fixed, but, rather, suggests that there are a range of possible futures and that in some way we may be able to perceive these possibilties.

This interpretation embodies a notion of time which is compatible with quantum physics and lies at the heart of those physical theories of precognition which fall back, in one way or another, on the implications of the Uncertainty Principle. If fact, it is much the preferred interpretation of most modern precognition theorists because it gets around the problems once raised by precognition for the existence of free will, (to be discussed in Chapter Twelve) and because it accords much better with the known details of most apparent cases of spontaneous precognition. It certainly accords with those cited earlier in this book, in each one of which the person who had had the precognitive experience seemed to be seeing something that he would later see in 'real life'. Indeed, there are no cases recorded in recent history (with the possible exception of some automatic scripts) where the percipient of the precognized vision did not later participate in the foreseen event or see some visual report of it.*

J. W. Dunnee, for instance, in *An Experiment With Time*, observed that the precognitive material in most of his dreams appeared to be things printed on the pages of books or in newspaper headlines which he was destined to read a few days later. In his study of the 35 reportable instances of precognition connected with the Aberfan mining disaster, John Barker noted, 'several dreamers claimed to be able to pin-point the scenes of their dream in the pictures of the Aberfan disaster which were flashed on television or appeared in newspaper photographs' (1, p.176). And in the case of Miss H. R.'s roulette playing, she reported that her eyes were always drawn to a number on the roulette cloth (i.e., the place where she would be seeing the croupier place his peg once a number came up), not to a number on the roulette wheel itself (where the actual future event would take place).

Viewing precognition as the prevision of a *possible* future event rather than of an *actual* one also accords with reported cases, and helps to explain certain difficult cases where an apparent precognition 'gets it wrong' – i.e., where the foreseen event materializes, but with some important aspect altered.

For instance, there was a number of cases cited in Chapter Two (pp. 34–36) where a possible future event was dreamt of and then subsequently prevented because of the dream: Susan B. Anthony's dream of a hotel fire that might have killed her; Mrs Warren's dream of the Vanguard crash that moved her to cancel her seat on the doomed flight; the passenger who refused to sail on the *Titanic*, etc.

William Cox's train crash statistics which showed that fewer people travelled on endangeed trains than on safe ones (p. 36) suggest that such preventive precognitive (or premonitory) experiences may be common and these, obviously, are experiences that relate not to actual futures that *do* subsequently happen, but rather to possible futures that *might* well have happened.

Precognition and Virtual Transitions

The first really detailed physical theory of precognition to be put

---

*This analysis appears to break down in instances of a detailed precognition of one's own death such as Lincoln's dream of lying in state at the White House. Such dreams or visions represent that grey area where precognition might be confused with an out-of-the-body experience.

forward attempted to develop the notion of a future perception of a possible future event (precognitive telepathy) by bringing together what was known about quantum indeterminism in the brain with quantum theory's analysis of virtual transitions thus linking a known perceptual mechanism with a level of reality where 'possible futures' exist as a matter of course. The theory was proposed in 1960 by Dr Ninian Marshall,* a young psychiatrist who had earlier suggested a quantum mechanical basis for telepathy.

Marshall's theory recalls that a sub-atomic system is always, at any given time, a mixture of possibility and actuality, the one tending to give way to the other over a wide range of probabilities. An elementary particle within the system, such as an electron, tends when disturbed to throw out 'feelers' towards its own future state when faced with the problem of adjusting to some new energy level. These 'feelers towards the future' (its virtual transitions) simultaneously cover all the possible energy states the particle might actually choose to occupy – i.e., they simultaneously act out all of the particle's possible futures.

Each virtual transition, then, is precisely a dip into the future, a future from which the particle then 'comes back' to live out whichever actual state it has chosen to settle into. The premise on which Marshall based his theory was that precognition could be explained if there was a way that the brain could 'tune into' these virtual dips into the future, and he saw the proven quantum indeterminism built into the firing thresholds of single neurons as a potential key to this process.

The gist of Marshall's theory was to make the leap from the proven ability of single neurones to respond to single quantum processes to hypothesizing that there are:

1. a means whereby single quantum events (virtual transitions) can band together to build up a pattern; and further;

2. a means whereby the brain could magnify these microscopic quantum patterns into macroscopic perceptions. He called these pattern forming and magnifying processes 'resonance phenomena', and likened them to the kind of resonance effects which exist between oscillating objects such as tuning forks, or window panes vibrating in 'harmony' with rattling railway lines. Phrasing his theory in terms of a Law of Resonance, he stated, 'Any two structures exert an influence on

---

*A similar theory was published 5 years later by H. A. C. Dobbs in the *Proceedings* of the SPR (Vol 54, 1965). Dobbs' theory differs from Marshall's only in postulating the existence of imaginary particles called 'positrons' which are assumed to travel backwards in time.

each other which tends to make them become more alike. The strength of this influence increases with the product of their complexity, and decreases with the difference between their patterns.'

Thus, if there is any similarity between pattern formations in the brain and patterns building up in the virtual transitions of quantum phenomena, the increasing tendency towards a pattern amongst the virtual transitions (the theory holds) is going to create an increasing similarity in the patterns being built up in the brain's reverberating circuits. This concept of resonance is similar in many ways to Jung's synchronistic notion that 'like attracts like'. An event (sub-atomic in this case) is thought to act like a magnet drawing others into its own 'vibes' and thus building up a pattern which mirrors itself.

As a quantum process lives itself out, its virtual states move from the possible to the more probable and then on to the actual – a real transition, which is the end product. If, Marshall suggests, the brain is sensitive to quantum level stimuli, then it follows that at some critical point where the quantum process is approaching a high enough probability to set up a pattern formation, it will cause a similar resonance pattern in the reverberating circuits of the marginally stimulated brain neurones – thus creating a precognitive image which mirrors the increasing probability of some quantum event pattern. The ratio of these precognitive images to actual events which then occur will be the same as the ratio between the probability of a virtual transition pattern and the later formation of a real transition at the quantum level.

Thus Marshall proposes a physical theory of precognition based on the brain's supposed ability to tune into the probability states of quantum virtual transitions and to experience, through resonance, a pattern formation which could mirror at a level accessible to consciousness any pattern formations amongst probabilistic quantum events – if these exist. While critics might easily argue that this is a very big 'if' which itself almost presupposes the existence of precognitive phenomena, Marshall's approach has several advantages. It lends itself to a simple quantum mechanical explanation of how a future 'something' can be seen now, though it has not yet happened; it fits in with what is known about brain functioning; and it can offer a tenable explanation for the randomness and inaccuracy which dogs so many reported cases of apparent precognition.

The contents of precognitive visions tend on the whole to be vague, a beguiling mixture of very accurate detail in some respects combined with fuzzy suggestions of a coming reality and some bits which bear no relation at all to the later, actual event. Such a confused picture is what might be expected on the virtual transitions theory since, if it is *possible* future perceptions which are being foreseen in precognition, we would expect there to be a great deal of indeterminacy involved. Since a virtual transition can only be described as a probability wave, any precognition arising from such an indeterminate quantum level event would be bound to mirror that indeterminacy.

Further, there are the many reported cases of 'near miss' precognitions where the precognitive vision (whether spontaneous or produced under laboratory conditions) displays an unpredictable tendency to 'shift' some features of the later actual event. In the Soal-Shackleton card-guessing experiments, for example, the data frequently showed that Shackleton had guessed not the *next* card, but rather the one after that or in some cases the card which had *preceded* his target guess.

Similarly, in the Stanford University remote viewing experiments of Targ and Puthoff, the subjects frequently described the scene that the assistants would have visited had they opened the *next* envelope to be selected by the random number generator, and Targ and Puthoff described these interesting misses as 'displacement effects'. Equally, in the report of Miss H. R.'s roulette playing, it was clear that she frequently found her attention solicited by a number which turned out to be adjacent to the number which actually came up on the wheel as though she were somehow 'tuned into' the more probable existences of numbers that might be selected rather than knowing exactly which one.

All of these 'near miss' effects are what might be expected if precognition arises from perception of a range of possible futures through contact with quantum virtual transitions, and thus they need cause no embarrassment to psychic researchers. Indeed, on this theory the near miss phenomena are at least as, if not more, valuable than 'direct hit' phenomena for understanding the physical basis of precognition.

The Observation Theories

In 1974, American physicist Evan Harris Walker published the first of what was to become a whole series of physical theories of precognition which have come to be known as 'the observation theories' (78). Walker's own original observation theory has been commented on, altered and added to by other physicists, including Helmut Schmidt;

and Walker himself has published several revised editions of the theory (48). Like Marshall's theory of virtual transitions, the observation theories take quantum physics as their starting point and, taken together, they have for the past decade dominated discussion of how precognition might actually work.

The main inspiration for the observation theories flows from what quantum theorists call the 'measurement problem' – that is, the problem of how it is ever possible for all the manifold possibilities described in the wave function of a quantum phenomenon to 'collapse' into a single, measurable event. How is it that possibility becomes actuality? Why is there a world filled with concrete objects rather than just an amorphous sea of infinite possibilities?

Quantum theory itself has no answer to the measurement problem, contenting itself with stating that Schrödinger's wave equation describes all the possibilities associated with a quantum phenomenon and that all these possibilities remain viable (the phenomenon is spread out through time and space) until the moment we look at the phenomenon with our measuring instruments. The act of measurement itself, for some unknown reason, randomly determines that which is measured. As Gary Zukav has written in his *The Dancing Wu Li Masters*:

> Without perception (measurement), the universe continues, via the Schrödinger equation, to generate an endless profusion of possibilities. The effect of perception, however, is immediate and dramatic. All of the wave function representing the observed system collapses, except one part, which actualizes into reality. No one knows what causes a particular possibility to actualize and the rest to vanish. The only law governing this phenomenon is statistical. In other words, it is up to chance (87, p. 102).

Yet despite the cool contentment with statistics and mathematical formalism of hard line quantum theorists (the Copenhagen school), the measurement problem continues to plague the philosophers of physics and those quantum physicists who hope to understand the nature of underlying reality. One dominant hypothesis about the problem, suggested by MIT physicist Eugene Wigner, is that consciousness collapses the wave function; that is, that consciousness is responsible for the world as we know it by virtue of its role in transmuting possibility into actuality.

Thus according to Wigner, the conscious observer himself, rather than his measuring instruments, plays the crucial role in bringing about that which he observes. The observation theories of precognition are derived essentially from Wigner's hypothesis, though they add their own necessary twist entailing a kind of retroactive causality.

In essence, Walker's theory of precognition suggests that the conscious act of forseeing a 'future event' has the effect of retroactively creating the very event which was foreseen. Consciousness, he says, has the power through backward causation to collapse the wave function to order, thus willing into existence verification for its own 'prevision'. That which is foreseen will turn out to be that which was thereby created.

Unfortunately, because the observation theories are presented in very complex and technical form, their finer points are not easily accessible to anyone other than professional physicists. But it is possible to understand the basic model they suggest by relating them to Helmut Schmidt's quantum-level precognition experiments with radioactive strontium-90 (see Chapter 4, pp. 71-73).

Schmidt's subjects were asked to press one of four buttons on his experimental apparatus, whichever button they pressed representing their guess as to which one of four lights would next be triggered by the decaying strontium-90. If they guessed correctly more than 25% of the time, Schmidt rated them as having some precognitive ability.

Now according to the observation theories, the actual mechanics of a correct precognitive guess in Schmidt's experimental set up were based on the subject's having influenced the decay process of the strontium-90 itself (or its associated random number generator) *after* seeing which light had been triggered to come on by that same process. In other words, the subject *first* saw the feedback of his guesswork (the flashing light), *then* retroactively 'fixed' the decay process to produce the very result he had predicted (see diagram). Such a mechanism suggests that the process we have been calling precognition is in fact retroactive psychokinesis – the mind working backwards in time to influence material forces so that they then produce the result already observed.

Walker himself extends his theoretical work on observation theories to speculate on what the nature of human consciousness would have to be like to be compatible with them. Essentially, he describes consciousness as a quantum mechanical state similar to that which exists inside superconductors and then says that the observer's brain links up, via his senses, with the external world to form one quantum

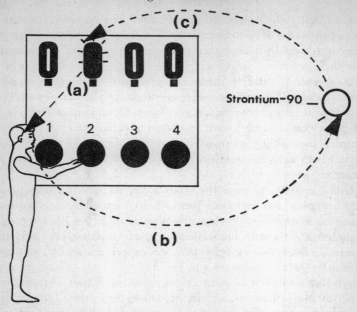

In the Observation Theories, precognition is interpreted as being retroactive psychokinesis: subject (a) sees the flashing light which verifies his guess that light 2 will flash next; *then* (b) he exerts a retroactive mental (psychokinetic) influence on the strontium-90 source which ensures (c) that it does indeed trigger light 2.

mechanical system (48, p. 311). Aside from being highly hypothetical, this formation runs up against the problem that, according to mainstream quantum theory, one quantum system cannot collapse the wave function of another, nor of itself. To get round this, Walker seems to suggest that 'will' operates as the *deus ex machina*, allowing the observer to collapse the wave function of an observed event according to his mood or intentions.

Despite the fact that the various observation theories have pretty well dominated theoretical discussions of precognition amongst physically inclined psychic researchers for the past decade, they have certainly not pleased everyone. Indeed, in the published literature their critics far outnumber their supporters. According to American philosopher Stephen Braude, 'the conceptual underpinnings of the observation theories are exceedingly weak at best, and the theories themselves seem largely nonsensical and lacking in explanatory power'

(10, p. 349). And Edinburgh's John Beloff, after pointing out that in the observation theories cause and effect 'chase each other in a temporal loop rather like a dog chasing its own tail', goes on to state that the necessary invocation of 'will' to explain the collapse of the wave function (the reduction of many possible futures to one actual present) means that they are not really physical theories at all (2, pp. 269–70).

Remembering the Future

At the 1974 International Congress on Quantum Physics and Parapsychology held in Geneva, American physicist Gerald Feinberg delivered a paper entitled 'The Remembrance of Things Future' (55, p. 54–73). His point of departure was a symmetry in Maxwell's equations of electromagnetism which suggests that, in theory at least, it should be possible to receive information from the future as well as from the past, and his purpose was to compare the common properties of precognition as reported and short-term memory in hope that each might shed some light on the other.

Such comparisons between precognition and short-term memory are becoming increasingly common amongst researchers whose work bridges the gap between parapsychology and physics and parapsychology and psychology. And while viewing precognition as a kind of 'memory in reverse' may not help to sort out some of the thornier questions in the physics of precognition,* it may illuminate the actual physiological mechanism by which such an ability could function.

Memory is something that everyone experiences as part of normal, everyday life, though not even the most recent research in brain physiology has been able to turn up a full explanation of how it actually functions. Still, for all their differences, memory theorists agree on one basic point – there is a definite and important distinction between short-term memory and long-term memory. Fortunately for our purposes, short-term memory is the better understood of the two.

Long-term memory is the ability to recollect data from over a long period of time. Memories from childhood, from last year, from last

*Feinberg's theory requires the existence of 'advanced waves', electromagnetic waves travelling backwards in time, and this approach has raised more scepticism than interest amongst fellow physicists. But a short-term memory model of precognition would, as discussed on p. 155, be compatible with the physics of precognition suggested by Ninian Marshall.

week, even from the last hour, would all be classified as long-term memories. Nothing conclusive is yet understood about how the brain stores and retrieves such distant bits of information.

Short-term memory, on the other hand, refers to bits of information available for recall for no more than a few minutes, and it is known that this function acts more like a processing mechanism than like a storage bank. The bits of information that the brain takes in and is able to retain for those few minutes are either permanently recorded in the long-term memory bank, or lost forever.

The distinction between long-term and short-term memory became evident when from observation of people whose brains had suffered temporary damage of a sort which interrupted normal brain functioning – people who had suffered concussion, had epileptic fits, or undergone electric shock treatment. In each such case, it was discovered that the individual concerned had no memory at all of the few minutes immediately preceding the shock to his brain, while his memory of more distant past events (long-term memory) was left unaffected.

In the case which most clearly established the distinction between short-term and long-term memory, part of an epileptic's brain was surgically removed in an attempt to stop the electrical short-circuits which were causing his attacks. The unexpected result was that the patient was subsequently never able to get beyond 'yesterday'.

It transpired that the patient's long-term memory of his past was left intact, as was his short-term memory faculty, but he was unable to transfer any information gained from new experience into his long-term memory bank. Any such information acquired was simply forgotten by the next day – as illustrated in an experiment where he was repeatedly shown the same newspaper, day after day, and each day he reread it with avid interest, always finding its contents new to him.

In looking at how the actual mechanism of the short-term memory processing channel works, we come up against the same questions that were raised in Chapter Ten, when asking how the brain might process precognitive perceptions. How, for instance, does the brain take bits of information from the external world and turn them into patterns which can be retained as thoughts or images? The clear advantage of looking at such a question in terms of memory is that, while short-term memory and precognition might well work in similar ways, a great deal more research has been done on memory. Also, for reasons discussed in a moment, memory would make a more reliable candidate for study than precognition even if we could produce precognitive awareness to order.

As discussed earlier, the brain is a complex mechanism of billions of electrical circuits. Information is taken into the brain when some external stimulus causes an electrical impulse to fire along these circuits, made up of neurones. The information taken in gets passed through the brain as the electrical impulse travels from neurone to neurone by the tiny electrical charges firing between the synapses (nerve endings) of the individual neurones.

The key to understanding that these electrical impulses passing along the neurone circuits lay at the root of how short-term memory operates was to be found in the nature of those incidents which erase short-term memory – concussions, epileptic fits, electric shock treatment, etc. All are phenomena which interrupt the normal functioning of the brain's electrical circuitry. If such electrical 'short-circuiting' could destroy the contents of short-term memory, it followed that electrical impulses travelling along the neurones must be the building blocks of such memory.

But given that such impulses were the key to the functioning of short-term memory, it still left the question of how image or thought patterns might be formed from such data. Each electrical impulse arising from an external stimulus lasts for no more than two milliseconds; yet the thoughts and images which make up the contents of short-term memory last for at least a few seconds, and perhaps for several minutes. Thus the brain must necessarily have some means for forming patterns out of these individual millisecond impulses.

The same problem of pattern build-up arose in discussing how individual, quantum-level precognitive stimuli might ever band together to form a precognitive image. And it is now generally accepted that short-term memory patterns in fact operate along lines very similar to the mechanism discussed when looking at Ninian Marshall's theory of brain resonance patterns in terms of precognition; that is, that these patterns are formed by reverberations (patterned vibrations) along resonating brain circuits.*

Like the ripple on a lake which circles outward from the point of disturbance in a patterned set of waves, thoughts and images take

*In fact, although Marshall's Theory of Resonance was discussed in terms of its possible usefulness in explaining the physiological basis of precognitive data processing, it was originally put forward as a theory of pattern formation in short-term memory.

shape in the brain's short-term memory mechanism by way of resonance patterns set in motion by the original electrical stimulus, reflecting and magnifying its message as increasing numbers of the brain's electrical circuits vibrate 'in tune' with it. If there are indeed stimuli available from the future as well, such resonance effects suggest a model of the brain deluged from all sides by the patterned waves of both memory and precognition.

THE SINKING OF THE TITANIC

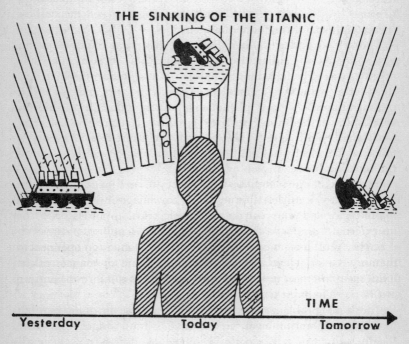

If precognition is indeed 'a memory of the future', we might picture the brain being deluged by sense data from both past and future. Here, the precognitive subject can both remember the *Titanic* sailing safely away 'yesterday' and foresee her sinking 'tomorrow', and both images are present in his brain 'today'.

Certain other similarities and differences between short-term memory and precognition are worth considering. Ample research on short-term memory, for example, has shown that recall ability falls off rapidly with time – indeed it falls off at the same logarithmic rate that was discovered by the Sheffield psychologist J. E. Orme in his study of the time factor in precognitive experiences. In Orme's charting of this factor in 148 cases of spontaneous precognition (see p. 73), the recorded instances showed a clear inverse relationship between the numbers of precognitions recorded and the length of time which separated the precognitive vision from the actual event.

But while short-term memory becomes increasingly vague with the passage of time until, at some critical point, the data disappear entirely unless they have been recorded permanently, memory does not show the same glaring inaccuracy and unpredictability that plagues precognitive awareness. If their mechanisms are basically the same, with precognition being simply memory in reverse, why this difference?

One obvious answer presents itself if we remember the probabilistic nature of the data with which precognitive perception has to deal. For while memory is a recollection of *actual* events or impressions, precognition is most probably a 'precollection' of *possible* events or impressions.

The brain, as we saw earlier, is subject to quantum level indeterminacies, and thus open to stimulation from the quantum virtual states of *all* probable events. Thus, if quantum mechanical approaches to the subject are correct, precognition (our memory of the future) would necessarily contain an uncertain mixture of 'memories' of actual events and 'memories' of lost possibilities. Such openness to quantum virtual states, which through neurone resonances might build up a pattern similar to that built up along the reverberating circuits in short-term memory, would be bound to make 'memory of the future' (precognition) less accurate than memory of the past. In many other respects, though, the two mechanisms seem very similar.*

---

*Some experimental studies have been done to test for a correlation between memory ability and ESP ability, but with inconclusive results (5).

12   Precognition and the Problem of Free Will

> Others apart sat on a hill retir'd
> In thoughts more elevate, and reason'd high
> Of providence, foreknowledge, will and fate,
> Fix'd fate, free-will, foreknowledge absolute;
> And found no end, in wand'ring mazes lost.
>
> *Milton*

The problem of free will has persistently dogged discussions of precognition, acting as one of the major philosophical objections to accepting that there ever could be such a faculty. Wouldn't the very possibility, it is usually argued, of someone's seeing the future before it happens necessarily imply the impossibility of his acting as a free agent with respect to that future? How is it possible, on the other hand, if we believe in man's capacity to act as master of his own fate, even to conceive of a future which is already written? And if the future is not already there for us to see, what can we possibly mean by 'foreknowledge' or 'prevision'?

Until recently, such questions have indeed led those who thought about them into 'wand'ring mazes lost', with no apparent escape from making a stark choice between freedom and prevision. No logical or physical argument seemed to offer any alternatives. But following so much discussion in the past two decades about the actual mechanics of precognition, perhaps it is now possible after all to get beyond this impasse and to find room enough in our scheme of things for both precognition and free will.

Before studies of precognition got so bound up with the complexities of modern physics as they are today, it was the fairly common view that if precognition were possible, its existence surely would lend crushing weight to the argument for determinism. In fact, this view seemed so axiomatic that advocates of free will rejected out of hand any seeming evidence for precognition lest they might otherwise be party to supporting what it appeared would be the final proof for the determinists' position. Professor J. B. Rhine summed up what seemed to so many this unavoidable pitfall (62, pp. 70–71):

> If precognition ever is or could be 100 per cent accurate, the knowledge of that fact would so profoundly affect our philosophy of life that one shudders at the implications. Especially is this true if, in addition, all kinds of events at any point of time are precognizable; for if they are, they are obviously all determined and inevitable. They would have to be fixed to be predictable. There would be no true freedom of choice. Even if a man knew by precognition that he would be in a train wreck, he could not avoid it. Of what avail would precognition be to the man in such a case? Evidence of such absolute precognition would imply a fatalism from which no decision could be truly free. Volitional freedom and perfect predictability are thus irreconcilable.

Of course the 'if' at the beginning of Rhine's remarks, as he points out himself, is a very sweeping proviso. For if precognition is indeed to set the seal on human volition once and for all, it would have to have at least a theoretical potential for 100 per cent accuracy. But so far, neither any evidence reported from spontaneous cases nor any data collected from laboratory studies of precognition has suggested anything like this perfect degree of accuracy. On the contrary, on existing evidence, precognition is such an inaccurate and unpredictable faculty as to give sceptics good cause to question whether it exists at all.

But when assessing the extent to which precognition might pose a threat to free will, the issue is not the known patchiness of precognitive experiences as so far recorded but rather the question of whether the precognitive faculty ever *could* be developed and controlled to produce predictions which achieved 100 per cent accuracy. And to this there is no certain answer. Much of the experimental research currently being done on precognition witnessed under laboratory conditions has this question of potential accuracy in mind, but until the actual physics of the faculty is thoroughly understood, it is unlikely that anyone will be able to arrive at a conclusive judgement. Thus it is still necessary to look at the consequences for free will in terms of both possibilities – the one, that precognition might potentially be accurate in every case if only we knew how to look for it, or the other, that precognition never could be 100 per cent accurate and is often given to error.

Earlier it was suggested that there are two very different ways of interpreting the nature of precognitive phenomena. On the one hand, what is being foreseen might well be some actual future event. On the other, precognition might instead be a foreseeing of the percipient's own possible future perceptions. Each of these interpretations lends itself to a different physical explanation for how precognition might work and also to a different conclusion about the relationship between precognition and freedom of the will.

If someone experiencing a precognitive vision is foreseeing an actual future event, then his foresight is likely to be explained best in terms of the static interpretation of time suggested by General Relativity. In Einstein's four-dimensional space-time continuum, the whole history of an event already exists, and each separate stage in that history is represented as a point on a stationary curve. As physicist Costa de Beauregard explains (20, p. 430),

> . . . relativity is a theory in which everything is 'written' and where change is only relative to the perceptual mode of living beings. Humans and other creatures . . . are compelled to explore little by little the content of the fourth dimension (time), as each one traverses, without stopping or turning back, a time-like trajectory in space-time.

If precognition were to be explained in terms of such a theory of time, then clearly very little room would be left to the imagination in drawing out the relevant conclusions with respect to free will. Foresight and fate are linked in such a view in the same uncompromising determinism which underlay the fatalism of the ancient Greeks. As was the case for them, there could be no freedom for the individual to shape his own future, no meddling with 'the records of destiny, massive tablets of bronze and solid iron', so unalterable that, 'you will see there the fate of your descendents engraved in everlasting adamant' (Ovid, *Metamorphoses*).

But of course, as we saw in the last chapter, the static time of General Relativity is not the only explanation for how precognition might work. A far more dynamic picture is arrived at by linking the faculty with quantum physics, and in particular with the inherent chanciness of fundamental reality as described in Heisenberg's uncertainty principle. A model of precognition based on quantum theory (as in Marshall's theory of virtual transitions or in the observation theories), where precognition itself is interpreted as a foreseeing of one's own possible future perceptions, would of necessity leave very little scope for determinism – and the outlook for free will would then be wholly different. As Oxford philosopher J. R. Lucas has commented (42, p. 108),

Quantum mechanics throws all the old assumptions into doubt . . . [The Heisenberg uncertainty principle] has attracted much attention. Some thinkers have claimed that it shows that even electrons have free will; more seriously, if it has been rightly interpreted, it shatters the argument from physics to determinism.

The fundamental reason why quantum mechanics shatter the argument from physics to determinism goes straight to the heart of Rhine's concern that if precognition were 100 per cent accurate it would necessarily conflict with the requirements of free will – and dispels any worry on that count. For a model of precognition based upon Heisenberg's uncertainty principle *never could* be anything like 100 per cent accurate in its predictions of future events, simply because those future events themselves are wholly indeterminate until they have been fixed in present reality.

According to quantum theory, then, the only future to which a faculty such as precognition could possibly have access is an indeterminate, probabilistic future consisting of all the 'might be's' packed into the Schrödinger wave equations. Thus the inaccuracy noted in reported cases of precognition would simply be mirroring the fact that in reality itself there is ample scope for any number of alternatives in the direction future events might take.

There is, for example, a rather well-known case reported by Rhine (62, p. 71) of a man who was planning to take a train journey the following day, but the night before he had a dream in which he saw his train crashing and himself being seriously injured. The dream caused him to change his travel plans and he was not injured, though afterwards he did read in the newspaper that the train he had intended to take did indeed crash. The case is often cited as illustrating one of the crucial paradoxes arising out of the inaccuracies of apparent precognition: since his dream was not wholly fulfilled by the unfolding of later events, how can it be said that it was precognition at all?*

A quantum mechanical model of precognition would get around this paradox by pointing out that there were in the first place any number of possibilities inherent in the situation described: the man might have ignored his dream, taken the train, and been injured in the

---

*There are many such cases on record where an apparently precognitive dream has led the dreamer to act so as to avoid the dream's fulfilment, i.e., Susan B. Anthony's dream of the hotel fire (p. 34), Mrs Warren's dream of the Vanguard crash (p. 35), the businessman who cancelled his trip on the *Titanic* (p. 36), etc.

crash, the train might never have crashed at all, or – as actually happened, the man might take such fright at his dream that he forewent his journey. Each of these possibilities, according to quantum theory, was equally valid until something actual happened.

Such a range of possibilities, which is not only compatible with but necessitated by the quantum mechanical model of precognition, is easily seen to be compatible with free will. Indeed, the evidence of several such reported cases of 'inaccurate' spontaneous precognition even suggests that precognition might be playing an active role in *adding* to our capacity to exercise free will by adding to our knowledge of alternative choices for the future. In the case cited by Rhine the would-be traveller, given his precognitive dream, was free to choose whether he would risk the apparent danger of travel or give up his travel plans for that day. Without that dream, he would most likely have been the victim of his 'fate'.

There is, however, a more subtle question associated with the quantum mechanical model of precognition and its suggested interplay between precognitive insight and the free management of one's own destiny, a question which bears as much on the nature of human personality as it does on the nature of physical events. This has to do with what is 'probable' as opposed to what is 'possible'.

In quantum physics, when an electron which has been circling an atomic nucleus in a stable energy state is disturbed, it has, as it were, 'its whole future before it'. There are an unlimited number of possible new energy states available to it, and it might settle down into any one of them. Thus, were we concerned with the free will of electrons, we might say that in determining its own destiny (future energy state), an electron has unlimited free will. But the interesting question is, to what extent does the electron actually exercise all that freedom of choice – and the answer is, not very much.

Bound up with the whole conception of probability waves as expressions of quantum events is the implication that as quantum processes proceed, patterns of behaviour tend to develop such that wide-open possibility very quickly gives way to probability. An electron which is totally free to choose from among an infinite range of possible energy states will in fact head for the most comfortable option – the energy state in which it will have to exert the least effort to carry on its orbital travels around the nucleus. Only a few of its possible new energy states will promise such 'an easy life', and only these few are among its probable new destinations. Thus the electron's theoretically unlimited freedom of choice is in fact greatly restricted by a tendency towards laziness!

The same distinction between the probable as opposed to the possible can be seen in terms of an example from the level of everyday reality. While the uncertainty principle might suggest that it is wholly possible for a writer's coffee cup suddenly to lift itself off his desk, float across the room and relocate itself on the mantelpiece, it is highly improbable that it ever would do so (because of the enormous energy expenditure required for such a feat). Indeed, it is so improbable that the writer need never seriously consider the possibility.

If we think about it, it seems very likely that human behaviour, too, is governed by something very much like probability functions. Just as the movements of disturbed electrons exhibit a patterned tendency to seek out resting energy states which accommodate their taste for low-energy living, thus limiting their otherwise unrestricted freedom of choice, the human personality also consists of a set of behaviour patterns resting on attitudes, neuroses, habits, etc. which are all too often designed to facilitate our getting through life with the least possible expenditure of energy. Following familiar paths, sticking to old habits, is so much more comfortable than the exertion of uncharted discovery, and it is necessary to consider the influence of this disparity when assessing the *actual* relationship between precognitive vision and the enhancement of free will.

Thus, while it might remain entirely possible that a human being who has experienced a precognitive warning *could* alter the direction of some future event through an act of his own will, it is important to ask whether any such action is *probable*. For instance, to take one obvious example, it is possible that a man heavily addicted to alcohol might suddenly give up the comfort of his bottle after having a precognitive dream in which he sees his wife killed in a car crash caused by his own drunken driving. But is it probable that he would do so? Unfortunately, our perceptual and cognitive habits are such that very few people would even take such a dream seriously, let alone exert the energy required to shift habits in time to take the preventive action required.

Given the existence of such probability patterns in human behaviour, Cassius's famous reminder to Brutus that 'the fault, dear Brutus is not in our stars, but in ourselves' looks less like an expression of faith in the existence of free will and more like a description of the limits set upon such freedom by man's tendency to behave in rather patterned, and hence predictable, ways. With rare exceptions human beings, in company with electrons, very seldom exercise the right to choose freely from among the wide range of possibilities held open to them by God or the uncertainty principle.

Conclusion

In the first pages of this book it was suggested that there is no hard and fast *proof* for the existence of precognition, no evidence of the sort which would convince an independent panel of disinterested scientists. Such a disclaimer may seem curious now when measured against the subsequent presentation of so many pages of what might be taken to be quite voluminous evidence of a very convincing sort, but it remains none the less necessary. While each dream or waking spontaneous case or set of experiments cited in the intervening chapters would certainly have its advocates, a sceptic might reasonably argue that no one of them, nor even all of them taken together, fulfils the strict criteria for firm scientific proof that some people are, in fact, privileged from time to time with advanced information about the future.

Nor, it must be granted, is the scientific case for precognition much strengthened in itself by analogies to certain effects exhibited in quantum physics or relativity theory, interesting as these may be. It is certainly true that the intellectual revolution wrought by twentieth-century physics has weakened the case *against* precognition, and it may even be possible, as we have seen, to use aspects of that physics for postulating how precognition might work, but evidence that something is possible is still not evidence that it exists. The sole acceptable scientific criterion for that would be the controlled production of precognitive data under repeatable experimental conditions; and so far no such data have been gathered.

But even if we are forced to admit that there is as yet no proper scientific evidence for precognition, are we thereby automatically condemning all the varied material of earlier pages to the realm of fraud or make-believe? Must it really be true that in every one of the many very different instances of alleged precognition cited the percipient concerned was guilty, in collusion with his witnesses, of either lies or wishful thinking? Most parapsychologists would answer a very forceful no to such suggestions, for at least two reasons.

First, it can be argued that the absence of any scientific proof for the existence of precognition does not in itself guarantee that there will *never* be such proof. If it does exist, precognition would not be the only one of our faculties which still eludes scientific rigour. For all of their conceptual advances, scientists still know very little about consciousness or the human brain. The full mechanics of ordinary perception, the functioning of long-term memory and the relation between 'mind' and 'body' are all still beyond the pale of scientific explanation.

But more importantly, many parapsychologists ask whether strict scientific criteria such as control and repeatability are in fact appropriate standards by which to judge the existence or non-existence of psychic abilities such as precognition. Those of a dualist persuasion would argue negatively on the grounds that such criteria are physical, and psychic abilities are by definition extra-physical. Others, even if subscribing to a materialist position, would say that such abilities are unquestionably bound up with a person's mood or psychological state and that so far we understand too little about such shifting psychological parameters to design appropriate scientific experiments which can take them into account. In a short essay on the problem of assessing precognitive data, Jung suggests yet a different reaon why science is not an appropriate tool for dealing with such matters (36, pp. 154–5).

> Anyone who expects an answer to the question of parapsychological truth will be disappointed. The psychologist is little concerned here with the kind of facts that can be established in a conventional sense . . . Naturally enough our scientific age wants to know whether such things (as premonitions, foreknowledge, second sight, hauntings, ghosts, return of the dead, bewitchings, sorcery, magic spells, etc.) are 'true', without taking into account what the nature of any such proof would have to be and how it could be furnished. For this purpose the events in question must be looked at squarely and soberly, and it generally turns out that the most exciting stories vanish into thin air . . . Nobody thinks of asking the fundamental question: what is the real reason why the same old stories are experienced and repeated over and over again without losing any of their prestige?

Jung's answer is that such stories are necessarily beyond the pale of disinterested science because they represent certain 'psychic facts', but as such they are for him no less 'true' than the objective facts of conventional science. Indeed, they are true in a more important sense psychologically than any objective facts could be. Thus for Jung, whether or not precognition should ever be proven scientifically to exist, or even be fully explained scientifically, is neither here nor there when assessing its psychological truth and importance. That importance derives not from the repeatability of data but rather from the constant repetition throughout 'the life of the centuries' of individual reports that precognition has been experienced. Such repetition, he argues, gives precognition an independent existence in the psychology of the unconscious, whatever science may say.

Given his disregard for raw scientific data in favour of spontaneous individual experience, it is little wonder that Jung believes 'the greatest and most important part of parapsychological research will be the careful exploration and qualitative description of spontaneous events' (36, p. 157). A good many old-style psychic researchers, alienated by the sometimes over-technical approach of experimental parapsychology, would be inclined, no doubt, to agree with him. But at the same time, they would be wise to remember that in his Theory of Synchronicity, Jung found quantum physics very close to what he regarded as the poetry of the soul. Both physics and the patient cataloguing of spontaneous experience are likely to play an important role in future studies of precognition.

Bibliography

Journal Abbreviations:
JASPR: *Journal of the American Society for Psychical Research.*
JSPR: *Journal of the British Society for Psychical Research.*
PSPR: *Proceedings of the Society for Psychical Research.*

1. Barker, J. C., 'Premonitions of the Aberfan Disaster', *JSPR*, Vol. 44: 1967.
2. Beloff, John, ed., *New Directions in Parapsychology*, London: Elek Science, 1974.
3. Beloff, John, 'Could There Be a Physical Explanation for Psi?', psychology: A Critique', *JASPR*, Vol. 73: 1979.
Scientific American, November 1979.
Science, 1974.
4. Blackmore, Susan, 'Correlations Between ESP and Memory', *European Journal of Parapsychology*: May 1980.
5. Blackmore, Susan, 'A Study of Memory and ESP in Young Children', *JSPR*, Vol. 50: 1980.
6. Bohm, David, *The Special Theory of Relativity*, New York: W. A. Benjamin Inc., 1965.
7. Bohm, David, *Quantum Theory*, London: Constable, 1951.
8. Born, Max, *Atomic Physics*, Glasgow: Blackie, 1969.
9. Boss, Medard, *The Analysis of Dreams*, London: Rider, 1957.
10. Braude, Stephen, 'The Observational Theories in Parapsychology: A Critique', *JASPR*, Vol. 73: 1979.
11. Campbell, Joseph, *The Masks of God: Primitive Mythology*, London: Souvenir Press, 1973.
12. Carrington, Whately, *Telepathy*, London: Methuen & Co., 1945.
13. d'Espagnat, Bernard, 'The Question of Quantum Reality', *Scientific American*, November 1979.
14. Dobbs, H. A. C., 'Time and ESP', *PSPR*, Vol. 54: 1965.

15. Dunne, J. W., *An Experiment with Time*, London: Faber & Faber, 1929.

16. Eddington, A. S., *The Nature of the Physical World*, Cambridge: Cambridge University Press, 1928.

17. Ehrenwald, Jan, *Telepathy and Medical Psychology*, London: George Allen & Unwin, 1947.

18. Einstein, Albert, 'Autobiographical Notes', in Schlipp, Paul, ed. *Albert Einstein, Philosopher–Scientist*, New York: Harper & Row, 1949.

19. Einstein, Albert, *Ideas and Opinions*, New York: 1954.

20. Fraser, J. T., ed., *The Voices of Time*, London: Allen Lane, 1968.

21. Freud, Sigmund, *New Introductory Lectures in Psychoanalysis*, 'The Case of Dr Forsyth'.

22. Gaddis, V. & M., *The Strange World of Animals and Pets*, New York: Cowles, 1970.

23. Gattey, Charles Nielson, *The Saw Tomorrow*, London: Harrap, 1977.

25. Geoffrey of Monmouth, *The History of the Kings of Britain*, London: Penguin, 1966.

26. Glass, Justine, *The Story of Fulfilled Prophecy*, London: 1969.

27. Godley, John, 'Dreams of Winners', *JSPR*: June 1947.

28. Gribbin, John, *Timewarps*, London: Dent, 1979.

29. Harley, Trevor & Sargent, Carl, 'Precognition in Dream and Manyfeld States', submitted to *European Journal of Parapsychology*.

30. Heisenberg, Werner, *Psychics and Beyond*, London: Harper Torchbooks, 1971.

31. Heywood, Rosalind, 'Apparent Precognitions by Juliet, Lady Rhys-Williams, DBE', *JSPR*, Vol. 42: 1964.

32. Inglis, Brian, *Natural and Supernatural*, London: Abacus, 1979.

33. Jung, C. G., *The Collected Works*, Vol. 8, London: Routledge & Kegan Paul, 1960.

34. Jung, C. G., 'Foreword', *I Ching*, London: Routledge & Kegan Paul, 1951.

35. Jung, C. G., *Memories, Dreams, Reflections*, London: Rougledge & Kegan Paul, 1963.

36. Jung, C. G., *Psychology and the Occult*, Princeton: University Press, 1977.

37. Jung, C. G., *Synchronicity*, London: Routledge & Kegan Paul, 1972.

38. Koestler, Arthur, *The Roots of Coincidence*, London: Hutchinson, 1972.

39.   Lambert, G. W., 'A Precognitive Warning of the Sinking of the Titanic', *JSPR*: June 1962.

40.   Le Vert, Liberté E., *The Prophecies and Enigmas of Nostradamus*, Eken Rock, New Jersey: 1980.

41.   Long, Joseph K. 'Extrasensory Ecology': *Parapsychology and Anthropology*, London: 1977.

42.   Lucas, J. R., *The Freedom of the Will*, Oxford: OUP, 1970.

43.   MacKenzie, Andrew, *Riddle of the Future*, London: Arthur Barker, 1974.

44.   Malory, Sir Thomas, *King Arthur and his Knights*, London: Faber & Faber, 1967.

45.   Marks, D. & Kammann, R., *Nature*, Vol. 274: 1978.

46.   Markwick, Betty, 'The Soal-Goldney Experiments With Basil Shackleton; New Evidence of Data Manipulation', *PSPR*, Vol. 56: May 1978.

47.   Marshall, Ninian, 'ESP and Memory: A Physical Theory', *British Journal for the Philosophy of Science*, Vol. X; 1960.

48.   Millar, Brian, 'The Observational Theories: A Primer', *European Journal of Parapsychology*, Vol. 2; 1978.

49.   Monod, Jacques, *Chance and Necessity*, London: Collins, 1972.

50.   Moss, Thelma, *The Probability of the Impossible*, London: 1977.

51.   Murphy, Gardner, *The Challenge of Psychical Research*, New York: 1961.

52.   *The New Scientist*, 'A Sense of Magnetism', Vol. 87, London: 1980.

53.   Nisbet, Brian C., 'An Ostensible Case of Precognition', *JSPR*, Vol. 49: September, 1977.

54.   Orme, J. E., 'Precognition and Time', *JSPR*, Vol. 47: 1974.

55.   Oteri, Laura, ed., *Quantum Physics and Parapsychology*, New York: Parapsychology Foundation, 1975.

56.   Pfleegor, R. L., & Mandel, L., 'Interference of Independent Photon Beams', *Physical Review*, Vol. 159: 25 July, 1967.

57.   Podmore, Frank, *The Naturalisation of the Supernatural*, New York & London: 1908.

58.   Podmore, Frank, *Studies in Psychical Research*, London: 1897.

59.   Prince, Walter Franklin, *Noted Witnesses for Psychic Occurrences*, New York: University Books, 1963.

60.   Rhine, I. & Rhine, J. B., 'Investigation of a Mind-Reading Horse', *Journal of Abnormal and Social Psychology*, Vol. 23: 1929, pp. 449–66.

61.   Rhine, J. B., & Feather, 'The Study of Cases of Psi-Trailing in Animals', *Journal of Parapsychology*, Vol. 26: 1962.

62.   Rhine, J. B., *The Reach of the Mind*, Pelican, London: 1954.

63.   Rose, Lyndon and Ronald, 'Psi-Experiments With Australian Aborigines', *The Journal of Parapsychology*, Vol. 15.

64.   Saltmarsh, H. F., *Foreknowledge*, London: G. Bell & Sons, 1938.

65.   Schmidt, Helmut, 'Precognition of a Quantum Process', *Journal of Parapsychology*, Vol. 33, No. 2, pp. 99–108.

66.   Schul, Bill, *The Psychic Power of Animals*, London: Coronet Books, 1977.

67.   Smythies, J. R., *Science and ESP*, London: Routledge & Kegan Paul, 1967.

68.   Soal, S. G., and Bateman, F., *Modern Experiments in Telepathy*, London: Faber & Faber, 1954.

69.   Spinelli, Ernesto, *Human Development and Paranormal Cognition*, Ph.D. Thesis, University of Surrey: 1978.

70.   Stapp, Henry, 'S-Matrix Interpretation of Quantum Theory', *The Physical Review*: 1971.

71.   Stevenson, Ian, 'A Review and Analysis of Paranormal Experiences Connected With the Sinking of the Titanic', *JASPR*, Vol. 54: 1960.

72.   Stevenson, Ian, 'Seven More Paranormal Experiences Associated With the Sinking of the Titanic', *JASPR*, Vol. 59: 1965.

73.   Targ, R. & Puthoff, H., *Mind-Reach*, London: Paladin-Granada, 1978.

74.   Tart, Charles, et. al., *Nature*, Vol. 284: 1980.

75.   Taylor, John, *New Worlds in Physics*, London: Faber & Faber, 1974.

76.   Taylor, John, *Science and the Supernatural*, London: Temple Smith, 1980.

77.   Thorpe, W. H., *Learning and Instinct in Animals*, Cambridge, MA: Harvard University Press, 1969.

78.   Walker, E. H., 'Consciousness and Quantum Theory', in *Psychic Exploration*, ed. J. White, New York: Putnam, 1974.

79.   Watanbe, S., Ueoka, H., Munaka, M., & Okamoto, N., 'Survey on Atomic-Bomb-Exposed and Non-exposed Twin Pairs: Pilot Cases Study from a Sociohistorical Viewpoint', paper presented at 3rd International Congress on Twin Studies: 1980.

80.   Watson, Lyall, *Supernature*, London: Coronet, 1973.

81. West, D. J., 'The Investigation of Spontaneous Cases', *PSPR*, Vol. 48: L946–49.
82. Wilson, Colin, *Mysteries*, London: Mayflower, 1978.
    14 March, 1980.
84. Wolman, Benjamin, ed., *The Handbook of Parapsychology*, New York: Van Nostrand Reinhold, 1977.
85. Wolstenholme, G. E. W., & Millar, Elaine, *CIBA Foundation Symposium on Extrasensory Perception*, Boston: 1956.
86. Yates, Frances, 'Oracle to the Cock', *Times Literary Supplement:* 14 March, 1980.
87. Zukav, Gary, *The Dancing Wu Li Masters*, London: Hutchinson, 1979.

Suggestions for Further Reading

Bohm, David, *Wholeness and the Implicate Order*, London: Routledge & Kegan Paul, 1960.

Brier, Bob, *Precognition and the Philosophy of Science*, New York: Humanities Press, 1974.

Broad, C. D., *Lectures on Psychical Research*, London: Routledge & Kegan Paul, 1962.

Lyttelton, Edith, *Some Cases of Prediction*, London: Bell, 1937.

Orme, J. E., 'A Note on the Nostradamus Prophecies', *JSPR*, Vol. 50, September, 1979.

Priestley, J. B., *Man and Time*, London: Aldus Books, 1964.

Saltmarsh, H. F., *Evidence of Personal Survival from Cross-Correspondences*, London: Bell, 1938.

Index